9/92

D1120041

The Beginning of Writing

Look for these and other books in the Lucent
Overview series:

The Beginning of Writing

by Lois Warburton

LUCENT
B·O·O·K·S

Library of Congress Cataloging-in-Publication Data

Warburton, Lois, 1938-
    The beginning of writing / by Lois Warburton.
        p.   cm. — (Overview series)
    Includes bibliographical references.
    Summary: Discusses the development of alphabets and writing
systems in ancient societies, highlighting Egyptian, Mayan, Chinese,
and American Indian societies.
    ISBN 1-56006-113-8
    1. Writing—History—Juvenile literature.   2. Alphabet—History—
Juvenile literature.   [1. Writing—History.   2. Alphabet—
History.]   I. Title.   II. Series: Lucent overview series.
Z40.W37   1990
652'.1—dc20   90-6010
                                                                    CIP
                                                                     AC

© Copyright 1990 by Lucent Books, Inc.
P.O. Box 289011, San Diego, CA 92198-0011

*To my daughters Vicki and
Gabrielle with love written
in stone*

Contents

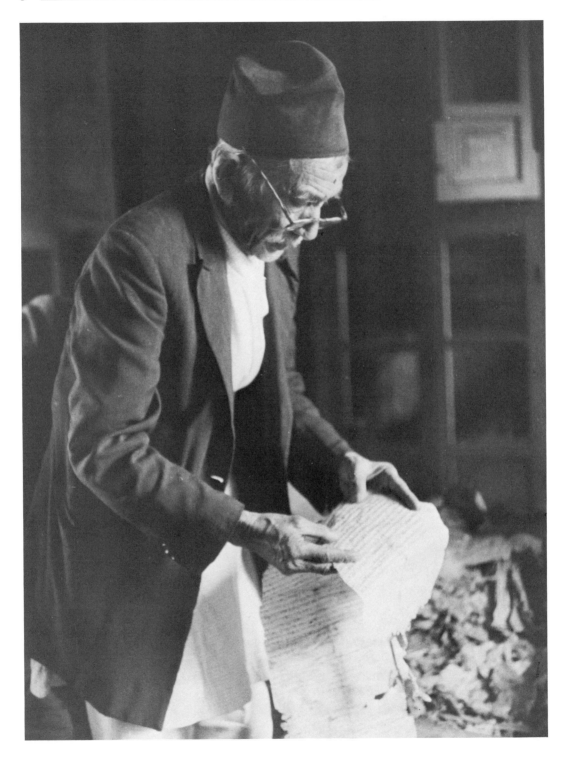

Introduction

THE ALPHABET is such an integral part of our daily lives that it is difficult to imagine life without one. But long before there was an alphabet, there were thriving civilizations of people who found ways to communicate with each other. Without an alphabet, however, their lives were very different. We can memorize the twenty-six letters of the alphabet and learn to write with them in just a year or two. Ancient people had to memorize thousands of writing signs and spend perhaps twelve years learning to use them correctly. Because of the alphabet, we can take written communication for granted. Our prehistoric ancestors could not.

What those people did when they felt the need to communicate in ways other than speech—to make visual records of their lives, their thoughts, and their possessions—makes a fascinating story. They had no one to teach them other methods of communication. For most societies, especially in the beginning, there were few examples to follow. These people faced a tremendous challenge, and they answered it with incredible inventiveness. The prehistoric artists who painted the lifelike cave paintings, the priests who carved the Mayan calendar in hieroglyphs, the Sumerian scribes who pressed cuneiform, or wedge-shaped, symbols into clay tablets: all these and many others found ways to communicate visually without an alphabet. This book tells the story of the

(opposite page) Whether in Nepal, where this man lives, or in the United States, written language enables human beings to record ideas, events, and achievements that otherwise might be forgotten.

9

Like children around the world, these Nigerian children learn to read the written language of their country in hopes of bettering themselves and their world.

communication techniques invented by these pre-alphabetic societies.

Only some of the techniques that will be described are defined as true writing. Many, including the cave paintings, the American Indians' winter counts, and the Incas' quipus, are examples of prewriting communication. None of these systems can be called writing as we know it, for that began with the invention of the alphabet. But all of these pre-alphabetic techniques have two things in common. The first is that they form a permanent record. The event, list, or whatever is being recorded has been drawn or written down so it can be remembered. The second is that, on the whole, these written communications are meant to be "read" by someone other than the artist or writer. A letter, for example, was usually meant for just one other person. Cave paintings may have been dedicated to the gods, or they may have told stories meant for the tribe. The hieroglyphic inscriptions on the monuments erected by Egyptian kings were meant for eternity and were addressed to all people throughout the ages.

The story of pre-alphabetic communications spans many thousands of years and includes civilizations from all over the world. It is a tale of mystery and beauty and, most of all, a tale of human creativity and invention.

1

The Mystery of the Cave Paintings

To MANY PEOPLE, the word *caveman* conjures up an image of a hairy, apelike man, swinging a big club and grunting. Most people think of prehistoric people as savage, stupid, and not quite human. But fossil bones found in the past one hundred years paint quite a different picture. Experts now believe that our ancestors, the first *Homo sapiens*, appeared on earth about 300,000 years ago. By 35,000 years ago, they looked much like people today and had brains the same size as those of present-day humans. In fact, if cave people appeared on the streets now, dressed in modern clothes, no one would think they were particularly strange. The life of these prehistoric people is a fascinating mystery that will never be completely unraveled because they did not have a written language to record it. Without a written language, they could not leave behind any records or explanations of their thoughts, feelings, and activities. In fact, the term *prehistoric* means "before recorded history" or "before events could be recorded in writing."

Prehistoric people did, however, leave other kinds of records behind for us to study. Their paintings, carvings, tools, and bones continue to be unearthed in sites all over the world. The problem is that the

(opposite page) Prehistoric rock paintings, like this one in South Africa called White Lady, *help researchers learn more about human history before events could be recorded in writing.*

13

These flint tools, arrowheads, and scrapers of twenty thousand years ago represent various stages in the advancement of human culture. By studying such remnants, archaeologists can reconstruct the lifestyle of ancient peoples.

meaning of these records is unclear. Scholars work to interpret the meanings from a number of different clues, such as where these items were found, how they seem to have been used, and how abundant they are. For instance, archaeologists have discovered the graves where our prehistoric ancestors buried their dead. From the bones found in those graves, experts have been able to reconstruct what those ancient people might have looked like. Animal bones discovered at cooking sites tell us what types of animals they hunted. Fossilized pollen found in caves reveals what kinds of plants covered the land these people roamed. The shape and workmanship of the stone and bone tools they left behind can tell scientists about how advanced their methods of cooking, hunting, sewing, and making weapons were.

By far the most amazing discovery has been the cave paintings these people drew inside deep, dark caves and on the faces of rocky overhangs. It is from these beautiful, lifelike paintings that experts have gained the most knowledge about the prehistoric world. For this reason, many experts believe the cave paintings must be one of the earliest forms of prewriting communication. The paintings are thought to have communicated information to the families or clans of their artists just as they communicate certain types of information to the experts today. But no one knows exactly what information the paintings were meant to convey. Pictures are not like writing. Written words express agreed-upon meanings, but pictures have to be interpreted, especially when the artist's intentions are unknown. So the cave paintings are still surrounded by mystery. Scholars do not agree on what the paintings mean. They do not know precisely why prehistoric people painted on cave walls. They will probably never know when or where the first painting was made.

The modern mystery of the cave paintings began one day in 1878 when Don Marcelino de Sautuola took his twelve-year-old daughter, Maria, to the cave that was on the hill of Altamira on his estate in Spain. He went there often because he was fascinated by the prehistoric stone tools he dug up from the floor of the cave. After a while, Maria became bored by his work and, taking her lamp, began wandering around the dark cave. Suddenly, she looked up at the ceiling and gasped. There, in the flickering light from her lamp, she saw a colorful herd of large animals. "Bulls!" she cried to her father, "Bulls!"

Colorful paintings

Don Marcelino thought she was seeing shadows, but he came to look. Much to his astonishment, the roof of the cave was covered with more than twenty red, yellow, and black bison, so lifelike in the flickering light that they seemed to be migrating across the ceiling. It was a remarkable sight, but the most amazing thing was that there had been no bison in Spain since prehistoric times. Excitedly, they began

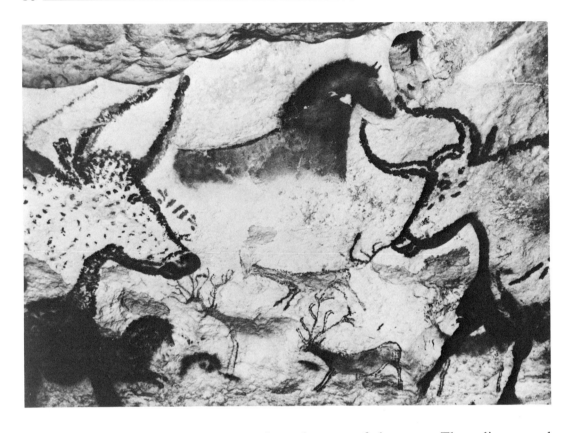

Ancient peoples often painted or engraved animals on rock, such as these depictions of deer, bulls, horses, bison, and mammoth found in caves in Lascaux, France.

to explore the rest of the cave. They discovered more and more paintings, not just of bison but of deer, birds, and boar drawn realistically and artistically. And along with the paintings, Don Marcelino found lumps of the ocher, which is red or yellow iron ore, and charcoal used to draw them as well as the stones on which these colored substances had been ground into powder. As he found more and more evidence, Don Marcelino became convinced that these drawings were prehistoric and the work of ancient cave dwellers.

Intelligent and sensitive people

Here was proof that prehistoric people were not stupid savages, struggling to survive, as everyone thought. The paintings showed they were intelligent, sensitive people who were expert artists. They were hunters who had intimate knowledge of the plentiful animals that shared their world. And they overcame great difficulties to draw those pictures.

Since many of the paintings are on the ceiling or high on the walls, the artists had to draw them while perched shakily on a foothold on the cave wall or on a companion's shoulders or perhaps on a crude, wooden ladder. And before they could begin, the painters had to hunt for natural minerals that could be used for paint, dig them up, grind them into powder, and moisten them into a pastelike substance by adding a bird's egg, melted animal fat, or blood.

In the deep, dark cave, the only light these painters could have had would have been from stone lamps or from wood or grass torches that filled the cave with choking smoke. They made the lamps by carving a bowl-like depression in a stone and then filling it with animal grease for fuel and perhaps moss for a wick. Both types of light were faint at best and constantly flickered. A cave artist rounding a bend in the passageway would certainly not have been able to see well enough to avoid running into the long, sharp claws of a waiting, giant cave bear.

Art that continues to move people

Despite these difficulties, the cave artists managed to create magnificent works of art that still appeal to people today. Sometimes they painted with their fingers, sometimes with hardened pigment shaped into crayons, sometimes with natural brushes such as feathers and frayed twigs; and sometimes they blew the paint through a small, hollow bone for a sprayed effect. The animals they drew with these techniques seem to come alive in flickering light, but the most animating technique they used was to incorporate the bulges and depressions of the cave walls and ceiling into some drawings. A round bulge became the shoulder of a bison, a hollow became the head of a horse. These three-dimensional animals appear

"Neanderthals, Neanderthals! Can't make fire! Can't make spear! Nyah, nyah, nyah . . .!"

filled with energy, as if they are about to leap off the walls.

The paintings were so magnificent that Don Marcelino could not convince the experts they were prehistoric. It was not until after Don Marcelino's death, when an increasing number of other, even more ancient, cave-painting sites had been discovered, that the overwhelming evidence convinced all the experts that the paintings were prehistoric.

Since that time, more than two hundred caves decorated with vibrant art have been found in southern France and northern Spain. Cave and rock paintings have also been found in such widespread areas as North Africa, South Africa, the Soviet Union, Australia, and the United States. But most of them are not as ancient as the paintings in Europe. In fact, some were painted in modern times by tribes like the Australian aborigines, whose culture, until the last fifty to one hundred years, was very like that of the cave artists in prehistoric Europe.

Primitive cultures

Actually, the term *prehistoric* is used in two different ways. Although it commonly refers to the period before writing was invented for the first time in 3100 B.C., it is also used to refer to any culture that does not have a writing system. By this definition, almost every culture, living or dead, has had a prehistoric period. Because that period came at different times for different cultures, both highly developed cultures and prehistoric cultures have existed at the same time for about five thousand years. In fact, there are still today a few isolated, nomadic tribes in places like Africa, South America, and New Guinea whose cultures have not developed writing and so are considered prehistoric. By studying some of these tribes, experts are able to learn more about how people lived thirty-five thousand years ago.

Scholars have spent many hours researching the

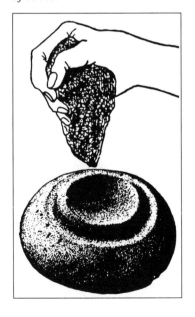

Cave artists probably carved bowl-like depressions in stone, filled the bowls with animal grease and moss, and then set the mixture on fire so that they could paint in the dark recesses of caves.

Until the last century, the aborigines of Australia lived much like the cave artists of prehistoric Europe. Researchers study their culture in an effort to know more about ancient humans.

cave paintings and the nomadic tribes that still exist and have answered many questions about our prehistoric ancestors, but one question still haunts them and always will. Why did those cave artists paint on cave walls, often deep in the cave, in the darkest, most inaccessible spots? It most certainly was not just for decoration, although it would have served that purpose very well. Too much of the art is deep in dark caves where no one could live.

Over the years, scholars have come up with various possible explanations. Most experts believe the cave paintings had religious or magical meaning. Many of those experts think the art was painted before a hunt as a magic charm to ensure success. They think the prehistoric hunters believed that drawing a

Researchers do not know for certain why ancient peoples painted animals on cave walls, like this one found in a cave in Lascaux, France. Some experts think the paintings had religious or magical meanings.

dead bison with a spear in its side could make such a thing actually happen later during the hunt. Other experts think the paintings were part of a ceremony or ritual that took place after a successful hunt, while still others believe the paintings expressed a worship of the animals the tribe depended on for its existence. All that is known for certain is that the paintings were an important part of prehistoric life.

The work of such scholars as Abbe Henri Breuil and Andre Leroi-Gourham of France has shown that cave artists thrived in Europe for about twenty-six thousand years, from approximately 35,000 to 9000 B.C. Then the painting stopped. Experts think they know why. The last ice age ended by 9000 B.C. As the ice retreated north for the last time and Europe got warmer, the vast herds of animals that had made hunting easy for thousands of years scattered and moved north. At the same time, the number of people increased, ever more rapidly. Hunting was no longer easy, and it became harder and harder to feed the growing population. Eventually, the struggle for survival left no time for art. So the magnificent paintings disappeared from tribal life.

Lively hunting scenes

Then, about 8000 B.C., a new type of rock painting began to appear along the east coast of Spain where another culture had developed. Animals were now scarce—bison and mammoths had completely disappeared from the area—but there were many people. They painted their pictures in the shelter of rock overhangs, not in caves, and most of the figures were human, not animal. The early rock paintings were lively hunting and domestic scenes, with people running, throwing spears, cooking, dancing, and tending children. Gradually, these paintings changed. In 7000 B.C., an artist might paint a scene full of energetic men running forward on muscular legs, poised with arrows in their bows. And each man was somewhat different, an individual who was probably recognizable to the artist's group. By 2000 B.C., however, the paintings had become more stylized and static. Artists were drawing men as stick figures that looked something like a cross with a triangular base. These figures no longer looked human, and none could be recognized as a particular individual.

These changes are important because they illustrate how written language can develop in any culture. Some experts believe that, gradually, over the six thousand years between 8000 B.C. and 2000 B.C., the artists realized they could use the picture of a man as an abstract symbol that represented the word *man,* rather than an actual person. At the same time, the artists used other pictures to symbolize things such as trees and animals. Then the figures slowly, over thousands of years, became more abstract and

In some early rock paintings— especially those depicting domestic and hunting scenes— various tools, cooking utensils, and weapons for hunting can be seen.

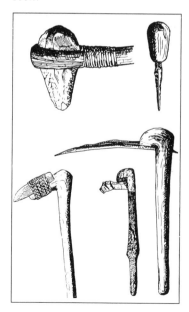

Depictions of people and animals gradually became more abstract and stylized, like these found in a South African cave. This led to the use of pictograms—a picture that consistently represented a particular word.

stylized, because it was faster and easier to draw simple stick figures. Whenever realistic or abstract pictures become symbols that represent words, they are called pictograms. All the first pictograms were pictures of people or things, tangible objects that were easily recognized.

Pictograms

Pictograms are actually picture words. Everyone familiar with the thing pictured can read the word. If a drawing contains a pictogram of a deer, it is meant to be read as the word *deer*. If there are three large stick figures and one small one, they represent the words *three adults and child*.

Pictograms are an important step in the development of writing because the recognition that a particular picture is used to represent the same word every time is the basic idea behind written language. Once that understanding exists, the pictograms can be learned and drawn the same way every time. This means they can be "read" the same way every time. Our writing is based on that understanding, but its stylized symbols are the letters of the alphabet instead of pictograms. The letters of the alphabet represent individual sounds of speech instead of whole words.

Although only one culture eventually conceived the idea of an alphabet, many cultures around the world invented pictograms at different times. Those in Spain are particularly interesting because they are among the oldest that have been discovered. The rock art was painted over a span of six thousand years and clearly shows a progression from realistic drawings to symbols.

Picture stories

The complete story of how and why this progression occurred will never be known. Perhaps when rock artists painted scenes from hunts, they actually were drawing the first stories. These paintings were picture stories. They differed from the drawings in the cave paintings because they told a story. On the other hand, a cave painting of a bison, for instance, simply indicated the physical presence of the bison and did not say anything about it.

No one knows for sure why these picture stories were painted. It might have been to thank a god for a successful hunt or to boast about the valor of the hunters. Or perhaps the painting was to remind the tribe of an important event, to leave a permanent record that would help them relive the experience whenever they wanted. But people from outside the tribe could not read the story accurately because it was only one artist's summarized interpretation of what had happened. It was as though the story had been written in a language that only the hunters and their families could understand. This was not a problem as long as people lived in small, isolated

Many cultures around the world, including the Anasazi of Arizona who carved these pictures, used picture symbols to tell a story or record important events.

Unlike the earliest cave drawings, which only depicted the physical presence of someone or something, picture stories actually told a story, as does this depiction of a hunt from South Africa.

groups, as our prehistoric ancestors did for thousands of years. Other groups might never see the paintings.

Better communication necessary

This situation changed, however, as the population grew. Not only were all the groups of people larger, but there were more groups. They lived closer together and ranged together over the same territory, competing for the same sparse game and the same grains, berries, and roots to supplement their diet. This would have meant more and more interaction among the groups. These groups would have needed to communicate among themselves in easier, faster, and more widely understood ways.

Since rock art appears to have been a popular form of communication, the artists most likely sought ways to make their picture stories understandable to people outside their own group. Abstract symbols that could be read by more people would have accomplished this. Also, the experts believe that as the population continued to grow, the food supply continued to dwindle, and eventually people had to use most of their time just trying to get enough food to

Hunting scenes, like this one found in a French cave, might have been painted to thank a god for a successful hunt, to boast about the valor of the hunters, or to leave a permanent record of an important event.

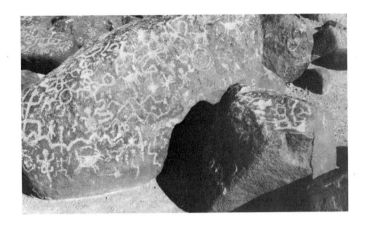

Rock art, like this sample in Painted Rock State Park in Arizona, often used symbols that could be understood by many people.

survive. The stick figures could have solved this problem as well. Now the artists could draw a hunter, as well as some other concrete things, in a few, easy strokes, in almost the same way every time. Unfortunately, much about these symbols will always remain a mystery. By the time these people had developed their paintings to this stage, their culture was already dying. There is too little evidence left for the experts to understand their use of these symbols in any detail.

If the rock artists had lived in a flourishing culture instead of a declining one, they may have had the time to continue improving their pictograms and to develop more of them. Then, if they had felt the need for an even clearer way to communicate, it is likely the picture stories would have evolved into the first type of true writing, picture writing.

In any culture, the transition between picture stories and picture writing was a slow process over a long span of time. Many drawings during this transition period contain elements of both, and the experts do not always agree on which form it is. In general, picture stories are a series of pictures that tell a story step by step from beginning to end, rather than being one realistic scene that recreated the main part of an event.

The major difference between picture stories and

picture writing is that picture stories cannot actually be read. The individual pictograms in a picture story can be read, but the story itself cannot. Picture stories are equivalent to the illustrations in a storybook. If we read the pictograms in a picture story, we would be reading a list of words, such as, "stone," "tree," "deer," "man." We would have read the pictograms, but in order to tie all those words together into a story and give it meaning, we would have to interpret the picture and fill in the rest of the information with our own words.

Picture writing, on the other hand, does not have to be interpreted. Its writers used pictograms to say what they wanted to say, word for word. Of course, the early picture writing of each culture consisted only of pictograms for tangible objects, and, therefore, the information was recorded in a very simple manner. If a tribal member wanted a record of the fact that he owned two horses, he simply drew two horses. We can read the pictogram as "two horses," much as we read the text in a book. That is picture writing, and its first use was a very simple form of record-keeping. Picture writing is considered more sophisticated than picture stories because it is more abstract and therefore can be "read" more easily.

No clues

The ancient rock artists did not have the time or need to take that step. In fact, about 2000 B.C., the rock art in Spain completely ceased. Perhaps the struggle for survival became too great and the people were wiped out by starvation or plague. Perhaps they were conquered by another culture and taken away into slavery. Or maybe they stopped believing in the magic powers of the paintings because of the influence of a more advanced culture. There are no clues for the experts to decipher. It is unlikely that anyone will ever know what happened for certain.

2

Memory Aids

THE BEAUTY AND MYSTERY of cave and rock paintings have made them the most permanent means of prehistoric communication, but smoke signals, bird calls, mirror flashes, drumbeats, and other such methods were also used. In fact, as the human population grew and scattered, and survival became more complicated, prehistoric cultures all over the world created many ways to communicate without a written language. Some of the methods they invented are still being used today by prehistoric cultures in Africa and New Guinea as their principal means of communicating over distance. Among the most complicated of these methods are devices called memory aids.

Memory aids are designed to help people remember something. They have been used all over the world in different forms. To a lesser extent, they still are in use. And many of these memory aids are examples of prewriting because they form a permanent record and are meant to communicate information to at least one other person besides the maker. Such devices can be as simple and small as a stone with a few straight lines painted on it. Pebbles painted with stripes and rows of dots thirteen thousand years ago have been found in southern France. No one knows their exact purpose, but it is easy to imagine a prehistoric tribe using them to mark the passing days or

(opposite page) As the human population grew and scattered, prehistoric cultures created new ways to communicate. In this nineteenth-century engraving, an Indian uses smoke signals to proclaim a successful war party.

to count the number of bison they killed. Memory aids can also be as large and intricately carved as the giant totem poles the American Indians of the Northwest erected to remind their tribes of their ancestry and tribal relationships.

But no matter how complicated or intricate they are, memory aids have a major shortcoming. They cannot be read by anyone who does not already know what they mean. They must be explained through speech by a person who knows the information they represent. The dots on the pebbles from France cannot be read by the experts because they do not know what information the dots were meant to record. A tourist in Alaska cannot understand the messages in a totem pole unless they are explained by a member of that tribe. That is why memory aids are considered prewriting, not writing.

These Alaskan totem poles, from around 1900, are examples of memory aids. The complicated, intricate poles cannot be read by anyone who does not already know what they mean.

The message stick is one of the most common types of memory aid used by prehistoric cultures. A message stick is a stick with notches carved into it. In Australia, the nomadic aborigine tribes used them to communicate with one another up until fifty years ago. If, for example, the chief of one tribe wished to propose a peace treaty to another tribe, he would send a messenger with a message stick to that tribe's chief. To do this, the chief would first carve the branch of a tree into either a small, flat slab or a small cylinder with tapering ends. Then he selected a strong, fast man to be his messenger. On the day the message was to be sent, the chief sat down with the messenger and told him the message bit by bit, while he carved a horizontal, vertical, or diagonal line into the stick for each important part of the message. After memorizing what the chief told him, the messenger carried the stick to the other chief and recited the message to him, using the marks in the stick to help recall each detail and showing the chief the meaning of each mark as he went along. The chief then had a permanent record of the proposed peace treaty. But that record was meaningless to anyone who had not heard the message.

The Incas and their quipus

The memory aid developed by the Incas was arguably the most complicated ever devised. The Incas were only one of a number of Indian tribes that lived along the west coast of South America. They developed into a powerful nation between A.D. 200 and 1440. Since this culture developed without a writing system, the facts about its past are buried in myth and legend. Most of what we do know was gathered by the Spanish after they conquered the Incas in 1532.

The Inca, as the ruler was called, had such a great need for information to help him conquer and control his empire that it seems amazing that his people

Although they tell a story, Alaskan totem poles like this one are considered to be precursors to writing rather than writing itself.

The Incas of South America were the only highly developed civilization in the world to evolve without writing. They lived in a rigid society and developed into a powerful nation with the help of fortresses like this one.

did not develop some type of writing system. It was the only highly developed civilization in the world that evolved without a written language. But even without it, the Inca and his bureaucracy ran the empire with a very tight fist. The Incas' society was very rigid. Everything had to be done a certain way, and it had to be done the same way every time. No one did anything without permission. There was little room for innovation and certainly no encouragement to invent something as novel as a writing system.

What did quipus look like?

What the Incas did invent was a memory aid called a quipu, and it enabled them to keep records of all the information they needed to run their vast empire. Quipus were made of string. Strands of string in bunches were attached at regular intervals to one long string so they hung down like mop heads. Each bunch was tied together at the top by a single strand of string called a summation cord. To record something, a *quipucamayoc*, or knot-keeper, made a knot in one particular string. The position of that strand of string, the color of the string, the placement of the knot, and the way the knot was tied were all part of the message. When one of the bunches was full of knots, the summation cord provided the total of all the information on the strings in that bunch.

Only trained quipucamayocs could interpret the knots, and their knowledge has been lost. The ancient strings of the few quipus that have been preserved are silent, and no one will ever know their

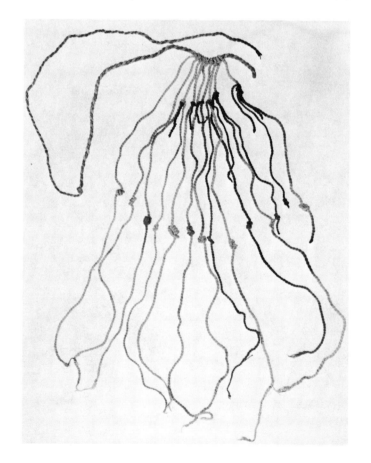

A complicated memory aid made of string, called a quipu, enabled the Incas to run their vast empire more efficiently. The string's color, along with the type and placement of knots, all had specific meanings.

messages. In the hands of the Incas, though, they were a very useful tool. The quipucamayocs consulted their strings to tell the Inca how many people could be spared from farming to provide labor for his many building, mining, and military projects. They knew how many baskets of grain, how many alpacas, and how many weapons the Inca had. Whenever a new tribe was conquered, the quipucamayocs went to their villages and took a census. From their strings, they knew how many villagers were male and how many were female, how many were young, how many old, and how many were farmers or herders or soldiers or medicine men.

Quipus were also used the same way message

When the Incas conquered another tribe as seen in this illustration from a nineteenth-century text, trained knot-keepers used quipus to take census counts in the conquered village.

sticks were used. Because the Incas did not have wheels or horses, walking and running were their only means of transportation. Special messengers called *chasquis* ran in relays throughout the empire, carrying the information the Inca needed to rule it successfully. Quipucamayocs knotted quipus for these messengers while telling them the message, just as the Australian aborigines did. The chasquis then carried the quipus on their relays to help them remember the message.

Quipus were once thought to be a form of writing, probably partly because they seemed so complicated and partly because the experts could not believe that such a highly developed civilization did not have a writing system. Experts now think most quipus were simply tallies of the numerous items the Inca wanted to keep track of—a form of numerical record-keeping. If the black strings, for instance, represented llamas, the knots on the black strings would tell the Inca how many llamas he had. Although quipus were used to keep tallies, they were not used to compute math. The totals were computed with piles of grain or pebbles before they were knotted onto the quipu. The quipucamayocs used a decimal recording system and had different types of knots to write ones, tens, hundreds, and thousands. Even though they understood the concept of zero, they did not have a knot that represented it. Instead, a blank space was left on the string.

The Spanish, led by Francisco Pizarro, destroyed the Inca empire in 1532. They also brought the Spanish language with them, as well as reading and writing.

Permanent records

While the experts think that most quipus recorded fairly simple numerical tallies, they believe it is likely the knots gave other information as well. The various types of knots in the black strings might also have communicated such information as where the llamas were located, how they were used, and how many were old and how many young. Unfortunately, no one can read them to find out. Experts also know that some quipus were records of the Incas' history, so a storyteller could consult his quipu if he could not remember the date of a battle. But no matter what kind of information quipus recorded, the fact that they formed permanent records of information that all the quipucamayocs could read makes them a form of prewriting.

For ninety years, with the help of their quipus, the Incas ruled their vast empire. Then the Spanish, led by Francisco Pizarro, arrived in 1532, and the em-

In this winter count, a Dakota Indian named Lone Dog has chronicled the important events involving his tribe between 1799 and 1870. Symbol number 71 at the far top left, for example, signifies the Dakotas' attack on a fort of Crow Indians.

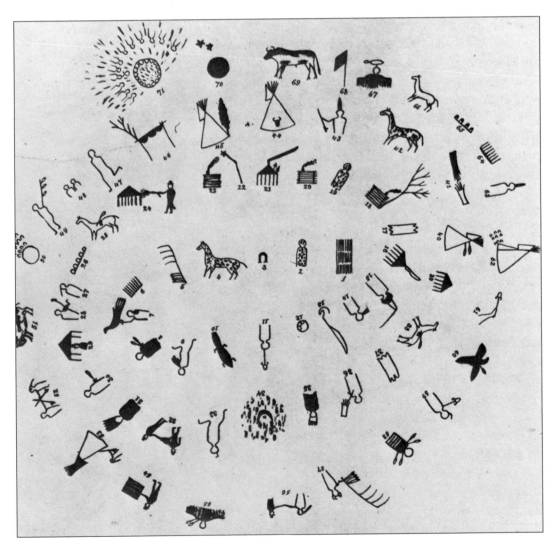

pire was destroyed. Within a short span of time, the primary language of that part of South America was Spanish, and those Indians who attended school learned to read and write in Spanish with the alphabet the Spanish had brought with them to the New World. But even today the remaining descendants of the Incas speak the ancient language, and a few of them still keep their records on quipus.

The North American Indians

While none of the North American Indian tribes developed a writing system, they did invent some very artistic memory aids using pictures. Some tribes developed those pictures into pictograms or symbols, and others painted picture stories, much as the prehistoric rock artists did.

The Plains Indians and their winter counts

To make a lasting record of things they wanted to remember, the nomadic Plains Indians—warriors from tribes such as the Sioux, Blackfeet, Crow, Cheyenne, Pawnee, and Shoshone—drew picture stories that showed scenes from important events in their lives. By advertising their exploits in this way, warriors could boast about their importance.

Many warriors drew what was called a winter count, because it was painted during the winter months. A winter count was a picture story of the past year in the life of a warrior, and it consisted of a group of simple pictures, each representing one of the year's important events. Sometimes it was painted on the deerskin that lined the inside of the tepees. Sometimes it was painted on a ceremonial robe made of buffalo hide so that the warrior's exploits would be visible every time he wore the robe.

For example, a young warrior who during the year had fought successfully in his first battle, stolen a number of horses from another tribe, had his first son, and killed more buffalo than any of the other

A Nebraska Indian named Sam Kills Two works on a winter count on an animal hide. The death of Turning Bear, killed by a train in 1910, is depicted on the second line above the artist's foot.

tribe's warriors would be eager to brag about his year. But before he could paint the pictures, he had to prepare his paints and tools. American Indians found and used many more colors but their paints were mixed and used much as the prehistoric cave artists had done thousands of years before. Red came from earth, clay, and pussy willow buds. Yellow came from buffalo gallstones and clay, blue from wild duck droppings, green from mud and plants, and black from charcoal and earth. These pigments were ground into powder and mixed with water and oil from a beaver's tail or buffalo hide. Charcoal sticks were used to outline the pictures, and porous buffalo bones, either broad or chipped to a point, were used for brushes to fill in the colors.

Then, with his materials beside him, the young warrior would sit on the ground beside a soft, smooth buffalo hide and decide what he could draw that would best represent each event. The victorious battle might be represented by a picture of him on horseback looking down on a fallen enemy killed by his spear. To show his success at stealing horses, he might again paint himself on horseback, with several other horses following behind. Since most warriors were not great artists, his drawings would probably be quite simple, perhaps even childlike. And they would follow certain conventions. For instance, the Indians drew things the way they knew them, not the way their eyes saw them. Perspective was entirely ignored. Men on horseback were drawn with two legs hanging down, as if you could see through the horse, because a man shown with only one leg might be doomed to lose his other leg in a coming battle.

When individual warriors painted their winter counts, they included as many pictures as possible. But it was a different story when it came time for the tribe to paint a picture on the deer or buffalo skin that displayed the winter count for the entire tribe. Every fall at the end of the summer hunting season, the braves of the tribe would gather to celebrate, and part of their celebration would be to add one picture to the tribe's winter count. The decision of what to draw was very important for the picture had to represent the whole past year in the tribe's life.

A successful hunt

If the hunting had been particularly good that year, the picture might show a successful hunt. If the warriors had won a big victory over an enemy, it might show them standing over their dead foes on a battlefield. If an old chief had died, and a new chief had been initiated, the initiation rites might be shown. The tribe's best artist would paint the chosen picture because this winter count formed a permanent record of the tribe's history.

The Plains Indians also used pictures to write letters and business receipts, although this probably did not happen until after they had been exposed to the culture of the white settlers. A warrior who sold a horse to another person for twenty-five dollars, for instance, might give that person a receipt on which he had drawn a picture of himself handing the horse over to the other person. Following that picture would be twenty-five identical marks representing the twenty-five dollars.

Some experts call these receipts picture writing, and the pictograms symbolizing dollars could certainly be classified that way. But the drawing cannot.

Iroquois Indians, such as Chief White Cloud pictured here, formed a council to settle disputes between the Iroquois and other Indian tribes. The council used a wampum, or belt made of shells, to record decisions and agreements.

It is a picture story. In the first place, the Indian artist probably intended it as a representation of the actual scene that occurred when he handed the horse over to the other person. It is doubtful he intended the drawings of the horse and men to be pictograms representing the words *horse* and *man*. But even if he did, the drawing cannot be read because all the pictograms say is "two men and a horse." The rest of the story has to be interpreted from the way the pictograms have been drawn.

The Woodland Indians and their wampum

The Woodland Indians in the northeastern United States formed the Iroquois League, which was made up of several related tribes, including the Onondaga, the Cayuga, the Mohawk, the Seneca, and the Oneida. They all lived in the same territory in what is today New York and Pennsylvania. This league was the strongest Indian political organization in the United States. It was composed of a council of fifty wise men called sachems who were picked by the older women of each tribe. Their job was to settle disputes between the Iroquois tribes. Later, they settled disputes between the Iroquois and other Indian tribes as well as the white settlers.

When a council meeting was needed, swift runners ran through the forest to summon the sachems to the council in Onondaga (in what is today New York), the Iroquois capital. Sitting around the council fire, they debated the issue at hand for hours, until it was resolved by unanimous agreement or they agreed they could not reach a decision. In time, the council became very much like the present United Nations, with the goal of uniting all Indians into one peaceful nation.

All the treaties and agreements had to be recorded, but the sachems did not have a written language. Instead, they used a memory aid called wampum to form a permanent record of the terms of each treaty.

Nomadic Plains Indians such as the Sioux, depicted here during a ceremony, also drew picture stories to record the important events in their lives.

Wampum was actually white and purple seashells that were drilled with a small hole and strung together into belts. As soon as a treaty was completed, a wampum belt was made to record its terms. A typical belt would be made of white shells with a series of pictogram designs made of purple shells strung onto the white background. Each of those pictograms was a symbol for one term of the treaty, and they were generally geometric figures like diamonds or circles or crosses instead of realistic pictures.

One of the sachems was appointed Keeper of the Wampum, and he had to have a phenomenal memory so that he could memorize all the terms of every agreement, using the designs on each agreement's wampum belt to jog his memory. He also had to teach all his knowledge to his apprentice in case anything happened to him. No one could read the designs unless they had memorized the agreement because wampum is a memory aid, not writing. But because it formed a permanent record of the league's treaties and was used to pass the knowledge of those treaties down to future generations, it is considered a form of prewriting.

The Iroquois League was destroyed by the white settlers before it could reach its goal of uniting all Indians, but the idea of the league itself influenced the thinking of the founding fathers of the United States as they tried to unite all the colonies into one country.

Porcupine quills

Wampum was not the only way the Woodland Indians used pictograms to record information. They had another, much more artistic way of making designs to celebrate brave exploits and record impor-

Wampum—strings of shells used to record treaties—was highly prized by the Woodland Indians.

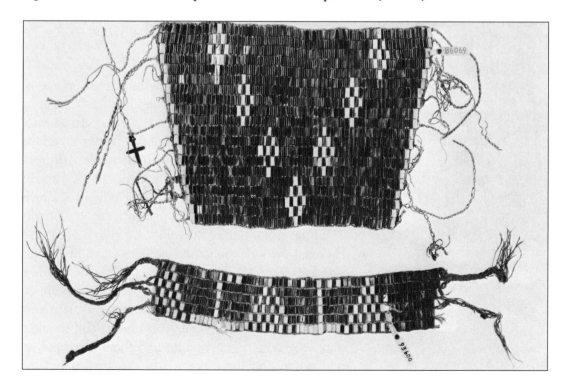

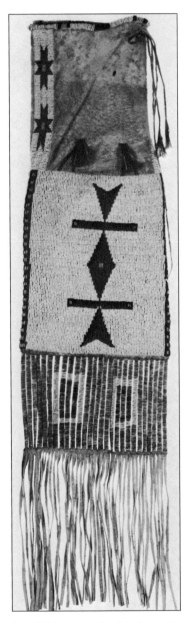

In addition to embroidering with porcupine quills, some tribes also used beads, as on this American Indian satchel, to tell stories.

tant events in their lives. This one was so beautiful that it was adopted by the Plains Indians and has now become a part of museum collections. The Indians used porcupine quills to embroider designs onto their clothing. The art of quill embroidery is at least several thousand years old and was a true Native American craft since it has been found nowhere else on earth.

The quill embroidery on the Plains Indians' deerskin moccasins and shirts served a purpose similar to that of the picture stories on their ceremonial buffalo robes: it recorded events and gave information to other tribal members. In some tribes, for instance, if a warrior had all black quills on one moccasin and all red on the other, the black meant that he had lost a relative in a battle, and the red meant that he himself had been wounded. If another warrior's moccasin had a white band of quills around them and the band contained diamond-like pictograms made of blue quills, the tribe knew that each diamond represented a horse this warrior had stolen from an enemy.

Natural dyes

Making the designs was a long, slow process. Since porcupine quills are white, they first had to be dyed. Red from buffalo berries, yellow from wild sunflowers, and black from wild grapes were the most popular colors. The women made different shades of these colors by boiling the quills with the plants for varying lengths of time. When the quills were dry, they were flattened with a stone or bone. Then the women drew the outline of the design with charcoal on a deerskin shirt or moccasin and made tiny rows of stitching, about a quarter of an inch apart, inside the outline. Now, the women were finally ready to embroider with the quills. Putting several in their mouths to keep them moist and flexible, they wove them one by one into the stitching, over one stitch, under the next, over the next, under the next, until the quill was held tightly in place. Each quill was attached this way until the design was complete. Soon the quills were dry and stiff again, so they did not fall out. After the white settlers came, the Indian women began using beads imported from Europe to form the same designs.

Although many of the memory aids used by prehistoric, nomadic cultures were inventive forms of prewriting, none of them developed into writing. The reasons for this are complex, but most anthropologists believe that cultures must develop in certain ways before they can develop a form of writing. The first culture to develop a form of writing reveals why these conditions are necessary.

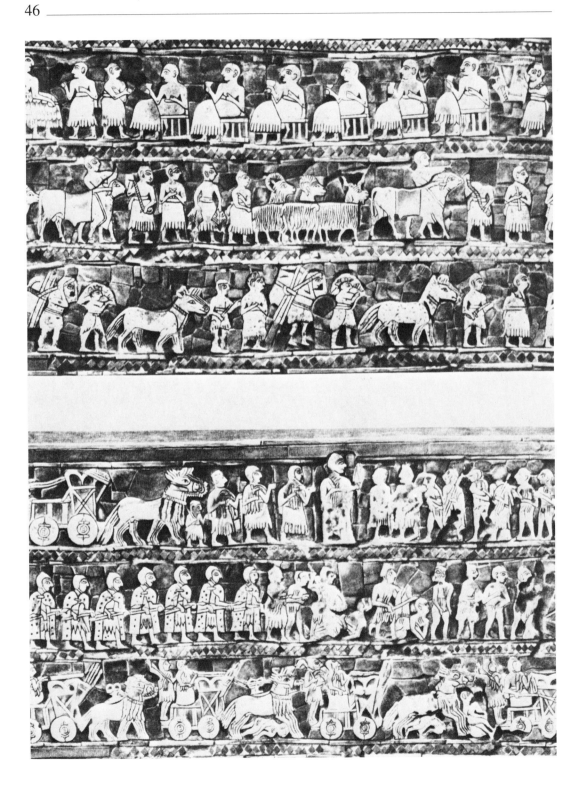

3

Why Writing Developed

A WRITING SYSTEM seems like a simple idea to people who have always had one. But nomadic cultures did not think of using symbols to write words that were meant to be read because coming up with that concept required a mixture of innovative cultural climate, intellectual curiosity and sophistication, and a real need for writing that those cultures did not have. Need is the most critical factor. Almost every invention is made in response to a need, and the invention of writing was no different. The need for writing was brought about by the development of civilization.

When scholars use the term *civilization,* they are referring to societies that have cities, social classes, well-organized governments, armies, a system of law, a system of money, large public engineering projects such as roads and water systems, and a number of specialized crafts such as metalworking, pottery, and weaving. In order for such societies to develop, people had to stop being nomadic and settle down in one place.

Sometime between 9000 and 8000 B.C., when survival had become difficult for the prehistoric, nomadic hunters on the European and Asian continents, some enterprising people in the Middle East

(opposite page) The ancient Sumerians invented money, the wheel, the plow, and methods for making bronze. They also may have invented the world's first true writing, in the form of picture writing, as seen in this Sumerian wall mosaic from around 2600 B.C.

47

took the first major step toward civilization. They domesticated sheep, goats, and cattle. They arranged to have a steady supply of meat, milk, wool, and hides, and life became easier, but it was still nomadic.

The next step they took was even more important, and it changed their way of life forever. Sometime between 8000 and 7000 B.C., a group of those people cultivated the first crop of wheat and became the first farmers. Farming created an entirely new way of living. Now they had no reason to move from one spot to another to find grain to make their bread and feed their herds. They settled down in one location, and gradually, over several thousand years, they learned to build better homes and improve their farming techniques. They also began to acquire private property and personal possessions, something that was impossible when they were nomads.

The beginning of civilization

As the population increased so did the farmers' ability to produce crops, and after a time the farmers were producing surplus food. Then some people realized that they could earn a living by making pottery or building boats and trading their products for that surplus food. Sometime after 5000 B.C., these people began to settle in villages that grew up along the riverbanks of the Tigris and Euphrates rivers in the land called Sumer that is now part of the country of Iraq. It was those small Sumerian farming villages that marked the beginning of civilization as we know it.

With civilization came the need for individuals to have a way to identify their property to themselves and others. The Sumerians designed pictograms, drew them on small lumps of clay, and poked a hole through the top. When the clay dried, they hung them as property marks on their cattle, sheep, plows, and wells, just as ranchers put brands on their cattle.

Sometimes the marks were pictures of objects and sometimes they were decorative designs. These pictograms were examples of prewriting, similar to the prewriting pictograms developed by other cultures.

Sumerian inventions

Between 3500 and 3000 B.C., the Sumerians invented money, the wheel, and the plow and discovered how to make bronze. They built many cities, constructed huge temples, and devised an intricate system of irrigation canals for the dry plains so that farmers could plant crops throughout the land. To

Archaeologists have unearthed evidence of other ancient written languages in the Middle East. These inscribed tablets, found in Syria, reveal a language that was previously unknown.

coordinate and control all these projects, they developed an organized society that was divided into city-states whose rulers conquered as much of the surrounding land as they could defend and hold. Those rulers were the kings and priests who owned most of the land and rented it to the farmers. And of those two groups, the priests, who ran the huge temple erected in the center of each city, usually had more power because the Sumerian temples were the center of the cities' commercial life.

The priests controlled the banking, manufacturing, building, and trade activities conducted within the temples. Every day, cattle, sheep, oxen, plows, copper, woven cloth, slaves, and clay jars full of grain streamed in and out of the temples' stores and farms. Gradually, it became impossible to keep track of all the temples' business transactions by memory. What the temples needed was a record-keeping system that all the priests could read and understand. In about

A fragment from a Sumerian carving tells a story about an attack that occurred many centuries ago.

3100 B.C., the priests answered that need by developing their society's prewriting pictograms into picture writing. By doing so, they invented the world's first true writing.

Experts have always given the Sumerians all the credit for inventing writing because it was in Sumer that archaeologists found the earliest evidence of writing. But because our knowledge of prehistory can come only from the things we find buried in ancient sites, every time a new discovery is made, our knowledge changes. We can never be sure that what we have found so far has led us to the right conclusions. Examples of writing that may be even older than those found in Sumer have recently been discovered in other parts of the Middle East. If tests prove that these examples were created before the Sumerians developed writing, it might mean that writing was invented slowly by many cultures over a broad area and not by a few Sumerian priests. Prehistory remains a challenging mystery, but each new discovery brings us closer to the truth.

4

The First Writing

THE PICTURE WRITING invented by the Sumerian priests was the first system used to keep records of the temples' business. It was written with pictograms that were drawn in a fairly realistic but simplified manner. The pictogram representing an ox, for example, was just the ox's head, but the head looked like a real ox, with curved muzzle and horns.

In the beginning, the record-keeping system was fairly simple. The Sumerian priests formed lumps of clay into tablets about the size and shape of a soap bar and drew on them with pointed tools, probably sticks or reeds. When a farmer who rented land from the priests brought two oxen to the temple as a tax payment, a priest recorded the transaction by drawing an ox's head, and then under it he made two circles by poking the end of the reed into the clay.

True writing

The experts consider the ox's head and two circles to be true writing because they are pictograms that were meant to be read as the words *two oxen* for the purpose of keeping track of the temple's goods. The Sumerian record-keeping system did not require any more information than that. The priests simply put all the tablets recording items received during the

(opposite page) An ancient Babylonian document tells the story of a king granting land to his daughters and asking for protection from the goddess Ninais.

day in one basket and those for all the items paid out in another basket. At the end of the day, they added up the day's totals from both baskets and recorded them on one tablet. That told them how much they had gained and lost. At the end of a week, the week's totals were recorded on one tablet in the same way. Clay tablets were clumsy to handle and bulky and heavy to store, so by consolidating the totals on a daily, weekly, and probably monthly and annual basis, the priests made their work easier.

Picture writing seems primitive, but it works so well in some cases that we still use it occasionally for writing today. Modern people, for example, can "read" the little man and woman pictograms on the doors of public restrooms, no matter what language they speak.

Even though the first picture writing revolutionized the temples' record-keeping system, it had one serious shortcoming. The pictograms could be used to write the words for concrete things, but they could not express ideas. It was easy enough to draw a picture of an ox, but how can you tell whether the ox is healthy or sick, brown or gray? How do you draw the picture of a "week" or of "crying" or of "flight"? The Sumerians invented several ways to express ideas with pictograms. When pictograms represent ideas instead of concrete things, they are called ideograms.

Types of ideograms

One kind of ideogram appeared when some pictograms began to represent both the concrete things they pictured and one or more ideas that people commonly connected with those things. In this way, a picture of the sun, which originally was only a pictogram for the word *sun*, could now also be drawn as an ideogram for the idea of "day," since the sun and daytime are usually connected in people's minds. In the same way, the pictogram of a bird might also be used as an ideogram that means "flight." The pictogram meaning "bird" and the ideogram meaning "flight" were drawn in exactly the same way, but their meanings were different.

Another type of ideogram was created by changing a pictogram slightly. Adding seven marks under a pictogram of the sun creates an ideogram meaning "week." Seven suns equal seven days which equal a week. This worked well for a number of simple ideas. But what about the concept of "crying"? The picture of a teardrop might work, but it could also look like a number of other things. A better idea seemed to be to combine the pictogram for "eye" with the pictogram for "water." Combining pictograms allowed the creation of many more ideograms.

Shortcomings of pictograms and ideograms

Ideograms are so useful that they are still used today to convey ideas in cases where people might not know the language or might not even be able to read. The international road signs are a perfect example. Everyone who drives knows that the pictogram of a car means "car," so the designers of the road signs wrote the ideogram for the idea of "do not enter" by drawing a car with a big diagonal slash through it. Whether people speak English, French, or Spanish, they can read that sign. They also know that a bottle with a skull and crossbones on it contains poison. The most useful thing about writing with pictograms and ideograms is that these symbols can be read by anyone because they are not directly related to a spoken language.

But a writing system based only on pictograms and ideograms still has many shortcomings. Complicated ideas are hard to express, and the signs are often easy to misinterpret. It is impossible to form sentences or indicate grammatical structure, so it is often difficult to read, especially since no punctua-

In this Assyrian-Babylonian wall relief, scribes count the severed heads of slain enemies after a battle.

tion is used. The signs just follow one after the other for the entire length of the text. Also, there is no way to write people's names.

By 2800 B.C., the Sumerian priests had found the solution to these problems. They realized that a pictogram or ideogram could represent not only the object or idea pictured but also the sound of its name. The priests invented phonetic writing. A phonetic writing system is based on the sounds of a particular language. Generally, each separate sound in the language is written with a different sign. Those sound signs are pictograms called phonograms. In the English language, the sounds are basically represented by the letters of the alphabet, and we use those letters to sound out or write our words. The Sumerians did not invent an alphabet, so they did not use letters. Their phonetic system was based on syllables, largely because most of their words were one-syllable words.

In the Sumerian language, the word *ti* means both "arrow" and "life." After they invented their phonetic writing system, a picture of an arrow was no longer a pictogram to be read as "arrow." Instead, it was a phonogram to be read as the sound *ti*, so the sign could now also be used to write the word *life*. Then, once the priests realized that those one-syllable sound signs could be combined to form new words of more than one syllable, suddenly they could write any word, including personal names. The words were "spelled out" syllable by syllable, much as we spell out our words letter by letter.

Sumerian system resembles a rebus

If you are familiar with the word game called a rebus, you can see how the Sumerian system worked. In a rebus, pictures of sound-alike words are drawn in place of words for which there are no corresponding pictures. Using the Sumerian system, the sentence "I saw two bees" would read:

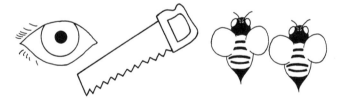

Words with more than one syllable were formed in the same way. "Horsemanship," for example, would be written:

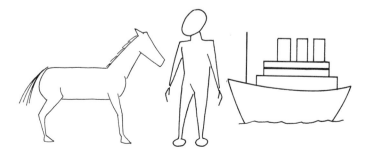

The invention of phonograms made writing much easier, and the few problems it created were soon solved. The biggest problem was how to differentiate between two or more words that sounded alike. We do not have a problem with words like *eye, I,* and *aye* because we use the alphabet to spell them all differently. But that is not possible in a syllable sound system because each one of those three words is only one syllable, and they all sound alike. The sound sign *ti*, for example, was written the same way for both "arrow" and "life." It was hard to know which way to read the sign unless the meaning of the text made it clear.

The priests solved that problem by putting warning signs called determinatives in front of sound signs that might be confused. The reader had to know how to recognize the determinatives because they were not pronounced during reading but told the reader how the word was to be read. For instance, whenever *ti* meant "arrow," the determinative for "wood," which was *gish*, was placed in front of it to let the reader know *ti* meant "arrow" and not "life." Since many words in Sumerian sounded alike, there were many determinatives to indicate such things as place names, personal names, numbers, girls, fish, and plurals. Believe it or not, determinatives are still used in the English language in the form of punctuation, although they have lost a good deal of their importance. The question mark is a determinative, and so is the exclamation point. "I believe." and "I believe?" have two different meanings. "I believe." is a definite statement of belief. "I believe?" means there is doubt.

Hundreds of syllable sounds

The main difficulty remaining was that there were hundreds of syllable sounds in the Sumerian language, and the priests had to memorize the phonograms for all of them, along with all their determinatives, before they could write. In the beginning, the Sumerians had about two thousand to memorize. Gradually, by assigning one sign to a number of similar-sounding syllables, they reduced the number to about six hundred, but that was still a great deal to memorize. Imagine that instead of simply memorizing twenty-six letters, you had to memorize six hundred.

This system of writing with syllable sound signs and determinatives seems complicated to us because we are used to writing with an alphabet, but it actually worked quite well.

Comparing ancient and modern classrooms

To see how it worked, compare an English lesson in a U.S. classroom today to a language lesson in an ancient Sumerian classroom. The lesson is to learn the words *bore, boar,* and *boor.* The U.S. class would first memorize the spelling of all three words. The Sumerian students would have to memorize only one phonogram picture. Then the U.S. teacher asks the class to write a sentence using one of the words, and one student writes, "The bore is fat." The teacher marks it wrong, because the meaning of the sentence is not clear. *Bore* in English is a noun that has several meanings. It can mean a boring person or thing, but it can also mean the hollow inside a gun barrel or a hole made by boring. And that use of "boring" shows that bore is also a verb, meaning to drill a round hole. In fact, it is also the past tense of the verb "bear." Because of those complications, the U.S. students have to learn grammar and punctuation before they can use words correctly. Grammar helps put words into context, and it is often from the context of a sentence that we understand the meaning of the words. Anyone who reads the sentence "I can't stand to listen to that bore" knows the writer means a person, not a hole in the ground or in a gun.

The Sumerian students have the same problem

An Egyptian wall relief from around 1350 B.C. shows scribes documenting important events.

with meaning, but their solution is different. Instead of learning grammar and punctuation, which they do not have, they learn the determinatives for all the different meanings. After memorizing the one syllable sound sign they use to write all three words, they must memorize the pictograms used as the determinatives for "gun," "person," "hole," "drill," and "pig." When they write, "The bore is fat," putting the determinative for "person" before the word *bore,* their sentence is correct.

Phonetic writing a rare accomplishment

The Sumerians' invention of a phonetic writing system was the last major step toward the later invention of writing with an alphabet. Inventing the concept of writing only with sound signs happened only two, perhaps three, times in human history that experts know about. The Sumerians did it, the Mayans did it, and maybe the Chinese. While it is true that phonetic writing may be a difficult concept to invent, one of the main reasons that other cultures did not invent it is because they did not need to. As the news of this remarkable invention spread, any culture could borrow the idea.

At the same time the Sumerian priests were developing picture writing into phonetic writing, they were also solving other problems with their writing system. Imagine how hard it would be to communicate in modern society if all we had to write with were realistic pictures. Think how long it would take to draw a good picture of the White House that everyone could recognize. And that would be only two words. The Sumerians encountered the same problem.

As their cities continued to grow, the traffic of tax payments, gifts, and trade in and out of the temples also increased. Drawing realistic pictures of things like sheep, plows, and grain began to take more time than the priests could afford, especially since they were trying to draw curved lines in thick, heavy clay with reeds. They needed a faster method of writing, and experts think it was their materials—the clay and the reeds—that encouraged them to develop as they did. In fact, experts believe it was the writing materials used in every civilization that determined the form that civilization's writing took.

Writing in clay

It may seem strange to write on clay, but in the treeless river valleys of the Middle East where Sumer was located, clay was the most abundant material. In fact, it was everywhere. All the priests had to do was go to the nearest river or canal, scoop up a basketful, wet it down with water, and then flatten and smooth

Because clay was abundant, it was a natural choice for a writing tablet. Pictured here is a scribe's writing palette from around 1450 B.C.

lumps of it into tablets. At the same time, they could gather the reeds that grew on the riverbanks, cut them into short lengths, and sharpen one end of each length to a point. The result was a reed pen called a stylus. It is fortunate for historians that the Sumerians did use clay because clay tablets, either dried in the sun or baked in an oven, do not disintegrate over time the way paper and wood do. Hundreds of thousands of ancient clay tablets have been found throughout the Middle East. It is by studying them that experts have been able to discover how the following improvements in writing evolved.

Gradually, the priests realized that it was much quicker to press the stylus into the clay than it was to draw with it. Sometime around 2400 B.C., they stopped sharpening the end of the stylus into a point and left it blunt or flat. Now when the stylus was pressed into the clay, the blunt end hit first and then the shaft, leaving a wedge-shaped impression on the tablet. Because of that shape, this writing system has

Sometime around 2400 B.C., the Sumerians began pressing their styluses into clay rather than drawing with them. This system of writing, evident in these tablets, became known as cuneiform.

become known as cuneiform, from the Latin word *cuneus* meaning "wedge."

Cuneiform eliminated the curved lines of the priests' earlier writing. The ox's head now looked like a triangle with one point at the bottom and two straight lines for horns sticking out of the top base. This made the pictograms less realistic and thus harder to recognize or read. To solve this problem, the pictograms were standardized. Every priest wrote each pictogram the same way every time. This meant that the priests had to memorize each pictogram, as we have to memorize the alphabet. Gradually, as they sought to write faster, they simplified the cuneiform signs until they looked nothing at all like the original pictograms. The pictogram for *ox,* for example, shows this progression:

Before the advent of cuneiform, the Sumerians used styluses similar to the one held by this young girl. The Sumerians made their styluses from reeds gathered at riverbanks. The reeds were cut short and sharpened to a point at one end.

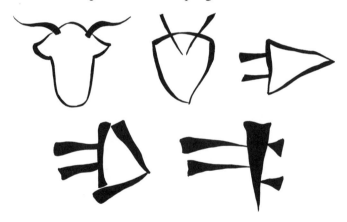

In order to make sure the priests learned all the signs properly, the temples invented schools. At first, only priests were allowed to attend school. Being the only ones in Sumerian society who could read and write gave them a great deal of power—it gave them knowledge the other citizens did not have. The priests wanted to maintain and increase that power as much as possible. But gradually, as business in Sumer became more complicated, the need arose for scribes, educated people who could write business contracts and letters and other legal documents like wills and property deeds. Soon, enterprising teachers opened private schools in every city, and upper-class and middle-class families began sending their boys to get an education. (Occasionally, a woman would become a scribe, but it was rare for a girl to attend school.)

Belonging to the scribe class guaranteed the successful students an excellent living, since the general population, including most businessmen, and even the king, was illiterate. They needed the scribes to

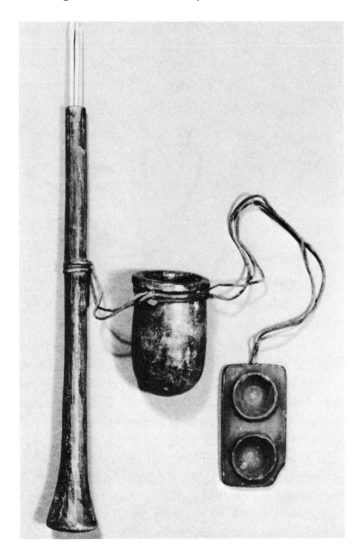

The tools of scribes from around 700 B.C., including a reed holder, a container of color, and a mixing palette, are exhibited at the Oriental Institute Museum in Chicago.

Thousands of clay tablets unearthed by Italian archaeologists in Syria may provide new information on ancient civilizations.

conduct business on both the private and government levels. A scribe might teach or administer a large estate or become a notary public, a civil servant, an assistant to the king, or a surveyor.

Scribes have power

Because they were almost the only ones other than the priests who could read and write, scribes also had a great deal of power. If a letter came for the king and only the scribe could read it, the scribe could decide exactly what message the king got from the letter.

In the process of conducting their business, the scribes introduced another interesting innovation sometime around 2000 B.C. They invented the envelope. The envelope, which was a layer of clay wrapped around the tablet, was invented to prevent

The Babylonians conquered the Sumerians and destroyed their culture, but built libraries for the highly prized Sumerian clay tablets. The most famous of these libraries was built by King Ashurbanipal, pictured here with his queen in a marble carving that appears in a nineteenth-century text.

fraud and permit privacy. Fraud was possible because most tablets were not baked, and therefore they could be moistened so the writing on them could be changed. The clay envelope was stamped with the seals of many witnesses, and if it were broken, the legal document inside could be declared null and void.

Most cuneiform tablets are very dull reading. The majority are record-keeping lists or legal and business documents. Other tablets, somewhat more interesting, contain religious literature, dictionaries, personal letters, and even notated music. The personal letters would be recognizable to anyone today. They contain phrases like "I hope you are well" and "Why haven't you answered my letter?" and "I love you."

Dull as they may seem to us, the tablets were highly valued by the Sumerians because they represented the sum total of the written knowledge of that day. For that same reason, they were also highly valued by the Babylonians who conquered Sumer in 1763 B.C. The Babylonians were from Babylonia, on the northern border of Sumer. When they took over Sumer, they destroyed the Sumerian culture. The

Sumerian spoken language died out, but cuneiform was adopted by the Babylonians and adapted to their language.

The Babylonians valued the clay tablets so highly that they constructed the first libraries to hold them. The most famous of those libraries was built by King Ashurbanipal. It held an estimated twenty-five thousand tablets containing between eighty and two hundred lines of writing each. Ashurbanipal was very proud of the fact that he could read, and he loved collecting "books." He sent people all over the Middle East seeking clay tablets for his collection. One of his letters to a royal official said, "Seek out and bring me the precious tablets for which there are no copies existing [here] . . . nobody shall refuse to hand over tablets to you. If you hear of any tablet or ritual text that is suitable for the palace, seek it out, get it, and send it here." The majority of his collection was writings on omens, astrology, and incantations, but there were also tablets concerning mathematics, astronomy, medicine, epic poetry, hymns, and songs. There were even some bilingual dictionaries of Sumerian and Babylonian.

The last cuneiform inscription dates from A.D. 75, which means that the cuneiform writing invented by the Sumerians was used, in various forms, for three thousand years. During that time, it was adopted by many other civilizations that recognized it as an answer to their communication problems.

5

The Egyptians

THE BEGINNING of Egyptian civilization was very similar to that of the Sumerians. By 5000 B.C., farming settlements were established all along the Nile River. Civilization in Egypt brought problems similar to those that arose in Sumer, but it was the growing government bureaucracy, not business, that created the need for writing. Because the Nile River flooded every year, the Egyptian farmers began to build dikes to keep the floodwaters out of the towns, basins to capture and hold the water after the floods receded, and irrigation canals to distribute the water to the fields. These projects required an organized effort among all the farmers, and a strong central government and bureaucracy developed to control and manage this effort. Eventually, this bureaucracy, with the king, the upper class, and the powerful priests in charge, became a huge, rigid network that managed everyone's life. By 3100 B.C., when the Sumerians invented picture writing, it had become impossible to run that network without an accurate record-keeping system.

(opposite page) The ancient Egyptians valued organization, art, and beauty, as evident in this famous bust of Queen Nefertiti, the wife of King Amenhotep IV of the eighteenth dynasty. The highly developed Egyptian society could not run without an accurate record-keeping system.

Writing from the gods

Long before then, the Egyptians were trading gold and linen with other countries throughout the Middle East. In exchange, they got timber, copper, perfume, and gems. While trading in the land of Sumer, those ancient Egyptian traders must have seen how helpful a written language was and realized how it could help their government's bureaucracy function more smoothly. They brought the idea back to Egypt, where it was quickly accepted.

The Egyptians, however, did not acknowledge this

Tuthmosis III so hated his stepmother, Queen Hatshepsut, that he had her name chiseled off all of her temples when she died. Although her likeness survives in this sculpture, the queen ceased to exist for the ancient Egyptians.

cultural borrowing. They believed that writing had been invented by their god of learning, Thoth, so they called it "words of the gods." Since written words came from the gods, they had magic powers. By carving a person's name on a tomb or monument, the Egyptians believed that they were helping to keep that person "alive." Erasing the name from those inscriptions made the person disappear. For example, Tuthmosis III hated his stepmother, Queen Hatshepsut. When she died in 1470 B.C., he had her name chiseled off all her temples, and as far as the Egyptians were concerned, that meant she had never existed. Words were so powerful that putting a written list of objects in a tomb was the same thing as putting in the objects themselves.

The Egyptians developed this gift from the gods into their own unique writing system, using the pictograms they borrowed from the Sumerians but drawing them in a very different style. Egyptian pictograms are called hieroglyphs. They were given that name in 300 B.C. by Greeks who visited Egypt. *Hiero* means "holy" in Greek, and *glyph* means "writing."

Egyptians valued art

Hieroglyphs were little pictures of Egyptian things and were more elaborate, more artistic, more accurately drawn than the Sumerian pictograms. Part of this difference is due to the fact that the Egyptians seem to have valued art more than the Sumerians. The Egyptians also had a more rigid society, one that was very particular about the way things were done. But the main reason for the difference between the Egyptian glyphs and the Sumerian pictograms comes from the difference in the writing materials used by these two ancient civilizations. Writing first on heavy clay with fragile reed styluses led the Sumerians to simplify their drawings. By the time the Sumerians began carving commemorative stone monuments some five hundred years later, their style of writing was well-established. The Egyptians first wrote by carving on stone. Carefully chiseling fine lines one by one into the stone enabled them to make each hieroglyph a sharply delineated, intricate, miniature picture that was decorative as well as useful. Once the design of a hieroglyph was established, it remained the same for as long as hieroglyphs were used for writing.

Egyptologists, or experts on ancient Egypt, have found and deciphered thousands of hieroglyphic writings. Although some mystery still remains, they now know a great deal about the ancient Egyptians and their writing. They know that the Egyptians, like the Sumerians, must have quickly realized the limitations of writing only with pictograms. Their population and business was still growing rapidly, requiring an ever more accurate record-keeping system. Moreover, the power of the kings was growing and so was their desire to glorify themselves, especially on the massive tombs they had built. They could not use pictograms to write, "The king triumphed over his enemies in a mighty victory." The priests, who at first were the only ones who could read and write, responded to this need by developing ideograms and then phonograms, as the Sumerians had.

Although the ancient Egyptians borrowed the concept of written language from nearby Sumer, they believed that writing had been invented by Thoth, their god of learning.

A closed, rigid society

While it is possible that the Egyptians borrowed the idea for ideograms and phonograms from the Sumerians, the experts think that is unlikely. Egyptian society was both rigid and closed, changing little throughout its existence and borrowing from other cultures even less. Adopting the use of pictograms from the Sumerians would have been a very rare exception.

Despite their rigidity, the Egyptians went one step beyond the Sumerians and almost invented an alphabet. Whereas Sumerian phonograms were all sylla-

ble sound signs, the Egyptians developed three kinds of phonograms. They had sound signs for whole words, sound signs for syllables, and, eventually, sound signs for letters. At least twenty-four of their hieroglyphs are phonograms for the sounds of individual letters, almost all of them consonants such as *W, B, M,* and *S.* Because the Egyptians omitted most of the vowels when they wrote, they did not need many vowel phonograms.

Egyptian hieroglyphs, like this one displayed in the Lowie Museum of Anthropology in California, were realistic, intricate carvings depicting Egyptian events.

Egyptians did not invent an alphabet

The reason the Egyptians are not credited with the invention of the alphabet is that these conservative people never did write solely with letter phonograms. They continued to write with a mixture of hieroglyphs. That mixture included pictograms, ideograms, word phonograms, syllable phonograms, letter phonograms, and determinatives.

The ancient Egyptians' conservatism is one reason they did not convert completely to an alphabet. But experts believe the main reason was that the priests and the scribe class that eventually developed in the business world liked keeping hieroglyphic writing complicated so that they could remain in charge of it. This gave them secret knowledge that helped keep them powerful. Over four thousand signs have been discovered, but eventually there were only about five hundred in common use. Still, to learn them required a great deal of memorization.

Inconsistencies in writing

The mixture of signs made it very difficult for modern Egyptologists to decipher hieroglyphs. It

Experts believe that Egyptian scribes and priests kept hieroglyphic writing complicated, as it appears in this sample, because it helped keep them powerful.

Egyptian scribes wrote vertically and horizontally, from the left and from the right and rarely spelled anything the same way twice. This complicates the work of deciphering hieroglyphs like the ones pictured here.

was also difficult because whereas the Sumerians scribes began to write consistently in long lines from left to right sometime around 2600 B.C., Egyptian scribes were never consistent. Sometimes they wrote their lines of hieroglyphs vertically, sometimes horizontally, sometimes from right to left, sometimes from left to right. A single document might contain writing in all those directions. And they hardly ever spelled anything the same way twice. Fortunately, they did stick faithfully to one rule: the front of the hieroglyphs always faced the beginning of the line. Whichever direction the person or object in the hieroglyph was facing indicated the direction in which the line of writing would read. In the picture below for example, the hieroglyphs read from left to right.

A third reason the deciphering was so difficult is the lack of vowels. If we wrote in English the way the Egyptians wrote, we would spell *car* and *care* and *cure* all the same, as *cr*. That probably was not a problem for the Egyptians. They knew their spoken language, and the determinative let them know what vowel to insert when they read it. But by the time Egyptologists were trying to decipher the hieroglyphs, there was no one left who knew the ancient Egyptian spoken language. So even though the experts know how to read hieroglyphs and can use the determinatives and the context of the writing to help figure out their meaning, they still do not really know how to pronounce or even spell them. That is

Ancient Egyptian scribes followed only one rule: The person or object always faced the beginning of a line, as in this sample of Egyptian hieroglyphic work.

why the name of one of their gods is sometimes spelled Amen, sometimes Amon, and sometimes Amun.

Hieroglyphs can be found everywhere

Hieroglyphs in all their forms have been found carved on tombs, temples, and commemorative monuments called stelae. But not all hieroglyphs were carved on stone. They have also been found painted on the walls of tombs and on mirrors, furniture, and jewelry. The Egyptians painted the words of the gods on almost everything, for the beautiful little pictures were both magical and decorative. With a fine brush and paint, they could continue the intricate, curved detail that had been developed first in the carvings. And then, sometime between 3100 and 2900 B.C., not long after the first hieroglyphs had been developed, they invented the perfect material for writing on. It is called papyrus and is almost like paper.

Papyrus was actually a reed that grew in many areas of the Nile valley. In some areas, this fifteen-foot-high plant, with its strong fibers and roots as big around as a man's arm, grew in dense patches along the riverbanks. Somehow the ancient Egyptians discovered a process to turn this reed into "paper." First, they cut the solid inner pith of the stalks lengthwise into narrow strips and laid the strips side by side on a flat stone in two layers. The second layer was laid crosswise to the first. Then they covered the strips with a cloth and beat them with a wooden mallet for as long as two hours until the strips were matted together into a single sheet. The sheet was left to dry under a heavy weight and then polished with a smooth stone. Finally, the edges were trimmed, and the sheets were glued end to end in a long scroll that was rolled up. The scrolls generally varied from 6 inches to 1 foot wide and 40 to 50 feet long, but rolls measuring up to 133 feet long

An 1875 rendition of papyrus, a reed that grew in the Nile valley. The strong fibers of papyrus provided a perfect material on which to write.

Most writing from ancient Egypt is preserved in the sacred hieroglyphic inscriptions on tombs, temples, and monuments, such as this decorated tomb in Thebes.

have been found. The word *paper* comes from the word *papyrus*.

The papyrus reeds also provided the scribes with their writing instruments. The end of a small reed, chewed until it was frayed, made a very serviceable brush. Red ink made from ocher and black ink made from soot, both mixed with gum to make them stick to the paper, were allowed to harden. Scribes kept little cakes of each on their ink palette and a little pot of water beside them. To write, a scribe would dip the brush into the water, then onto the ink, and then paint the hieroglyphs onto the papyrus.

Suddenly, an experienced scribe could zip through the hieroglyphs, much faster than an artisan could carve them on stone. And as the need for writing grew in government and business, the scribes began writing faster and faster. While the carved hieroglyphs remained the same, this speed brought about a major change in the hieroglyphs used for everyday business. In the same way the Sumerians refined their early, realistic pictograms into cuneiform that was easier and faster to write, the Egyptians fashioned their hieroglyphs into more convenient signs. The intricate details were transformed into fewer, simpler lines, and the lines were connected as they are in our cursive writing. The simplification continued until the signs written in this way barely resembled the original, sacred hieroglyphs (which were still used on tombs and temples), but they still had the same meanings. These new signs became an entirely separate and different style of writing called hieratic writing.

Much later, about 700 B.C., the scribes developed hieratic writing into a third style of writing that was a type of shorthand. It was similar to hieratic writing,

This papyrus roll from the Book of the Dead, dated at about 330 B.C., is illustrated with vignettes of great delicacy and beauty. It is about forty feet long.

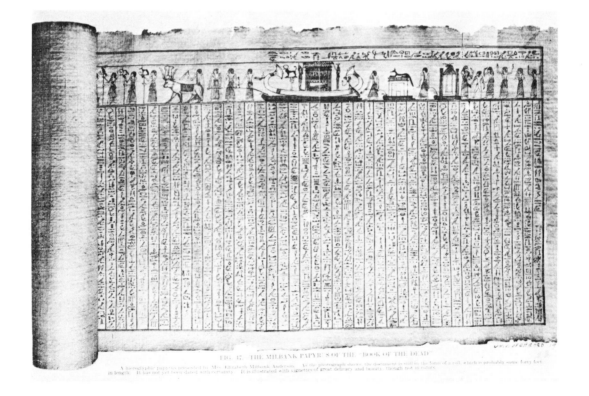

FIG. 47. THE MILBANK PAPYRUS OF THE "BOOK OF THE DEAD"

A hieroglyphic papyrus presented to Mrs. Elizabeth Milbank Anderson. As the photograph shows, the document is still in the form of a roll, which is probably some forty feet in length. It has not yet been dated with certainty. It is illustrated with vignettes of great delicacy and beauty, though not in colors.

but the signs were even more simplified. The main difference was that the signs were drawn separately rather than being connected. They still had the same meaning as both the original hieroglyphs and the hieratic signs they had come from, but they looked completely different. This style of writing is called demotic, which means, in Greek, "of the people."

The impact of demotic writing

Before demotic writing, perhaps only 2 percent of ancient Egyptians could read and write. After demotic writing appeared, most ordinary citizens in their daily lives could read and write. Although experts are not sure who is responsible for developing it, it probably developed because Egyptian civilization was declining. The priests, scribes, and king were losing their power, which enabled the common people to gain more power of their own. Literacy, knowing how to read and write, brings knowledge, and knowledge brings power.

Until demotic writing became popular, the scribes held a favored position in society. They did not have to pay taxes or perform manual labor on the king's projects. Indeed, they considered themselves superior to people in other professions, and many ancient writings make this clear. "Put writing in your heart that you may protect yourself from hard labor of any kind," said one. "It is greater than any other profession. There is nothing like it on earth," said another. Families encouraged their boys to become scribes because that was the only way they could better themselves socially and professionally. Egyptologists can find no definite evidence that girls were ever taught to read and write, although it may have happened in the royalty and wealthier families. In theory, the profession was open to all boys, but in actuality it would have been very difficult for a poor family to send a boy to school. Promising students were allowed to go to the elite temple school and

learn the sacred hieroglyphic signs. Those who learned their lessons well could become accountants, doctors, priests, foremen of various crafts, a private secretary, or a member of the government bureaucracy. Those who did not do so well could become village scribes who wrote letters and business contracts for the villagers.

Pictured here is the oldest private recipe book found in Egypt in 1872.

Scribes became authors

After much of the population had learned to read and write, many scribes found it hard to earn a living. The people no longer needed someone else to write for them, so many scribes became authors and published books for the people to read. Each book was handwritten on a papyrus scroll, and each was different even when the story was the same. The scribes misspelled words, omitted words, and changed words in their rush to finish the books and sell them.

Most of the writing preserved from ancient Egypt is in the form of sacred hieroglyphic inscriptions on tombs, temples, and monuments. Those writings have given us knowledge about the history, religion, and social customs of the Egyptians. But numerous papyrus rolls have been found that contain literature written in both hieratic and demotic forms. The earlier literature was not written to be read by the people. After all, until 700 B.C. or so, only 2 percent of the people could read. It was written to be placed in tombs for the pleasure of the dead in their eternal life. Since words were magical, it did not matter whether the dead person had been able to read when alive.

Some of the stories sound familiar to us today. For instance, there is the story of the shipwrecked sailor

Writings found in Egyptian monuments, such as pyramids, provide insight to the history, religion, and social customs of the Egyptians.

who set sail for the king's mines with a crew of 120.

He wrote, "A storm broke while we were at sea . . . the ship sank and of them that were in it not one survived but me. I was cast upon an island by a wave of the sea and there spent three days alone. I . . . made burnt offerings to the gods, whereupon I heard the sound of thunder. Trees fell and the earth quaked. I uncovered my face and saw a snake draw near. It was forty-five feet long, with a trailing beard, and its body was covered with gold."

There are adventure stories and detective stories and fairy tales. There is also love poetry. The following was written by a lovesick man who had not seen his beloved (whom he calls his sister) in a long time:

Seven days to yesterday I have not seen the sister
and an illness has invaded me.
My body has become heavy,
forgetful of myself.
If the chief of physicians come to me,
my heart is not content with their cures.
The . . . priests, no way out is in them.
My sickness will not be diagnosed.

Napoleon's soldier finds a clue

We would not be able to enjoy this literature today if it were not for a soldier in Napoleon's army. The last hieroglyphic inscription dates from A.D. 394. About that time, the ancient Egyptian language died out and with it the knowledge of hieroglyphic writing. Despite many attempts to decipher it, the hieroglyphic writing remained a mystery for almost fifteen hundred years, until Napoleon invaded Egypt in 1799. One day, while digging a fort on the Rosetta branch of the Nile, one of Napoleon's soldiers found a black stone with writing carved on it. It was quite different from the other stones he had seen. This one was covered with what seemed to be three different kinds of writing. Thinking it must be important, the soldier brought it to the attention of his superiors. They made plaster casts of the in-

scriptions and sent them out to all interested experts. The soldier had been correct. The Rosetta stone, as it came to be called, was the key to deciphering the ancient hieroglyphs because the inscription had been written in Greek as well as in hieroglyphs and in demotic writing.

The Rosetta stone did not yield up its secrets easily. It was not until 1822 that thirty-two-year-old Jean Champollion, a French genius who, it is said, swore at the age of eleven that he would be the first to read hieroglyphs, finally solved the mystery. The first hieroglyphs he deciphered spelled out the names of two rulers, Cleopatra and Ptolemy.

During all the years the hieroglyphs remained a mystery, another ancient form of writing was still going strong. It is, in fact, still being used today. That writing system developed in China.

(opposite page) The Rosetta stone, discovered in 1799 by one of Napoleon Bonaparte's soldiers, enabled Egyptologists to decipher the hieroglyphs left behind by the ancient Egyptians.

6

The Chinese

THE CHINESE were farmers in the Yellow River Valley in 4500 B.C., and their civilization grew up between 1766 and 1122 B.C. At the center of that civilization was a complicated, powerful religion, and it was that religion that first brought about the need for writing.

China was, and still is, a vast, diverse country. The Chinese people belong to more than fifty different cultures, each speaking its own dialect of the Chinese language. Dialects differ not only in how words are pronounced, they also usually have partly different vocabularies. In many cases, people who speak different dialects cannot understand one another. Each Chinese culture was generally centered in a different region of the country, and its people did not associate with people from other cultures any more than necessary. But they did all have one thing in common, and that was their religion.

To the Chinese everything in life depended on the goodwill of the gods and ancestral spirits. That is why the emperor's main duty was to intercede with the gods on behalf of all his people. He did this by asking the gods what to do about everything, from when to plant rice to when to go to war. The Chinese believed the gods would listen to the emperor because he was a powerful man. But the emperor needed a way to keep track of the gods' answers to

(opposite page) Classic Chinese writing, like that done by this Chinese artist, evolved from an early form of Chinese picture writing around 1500 B.C.

the thousands of questions he asked.

Picture writing was the solution, and it appeared quite suddenly in China in about 1500 B.C. Since experts cannot find any evidence of the earlier development that led to this writing, as they can for other cultures, its sudden appearance poses a mystery. Many experts think the Chinese borrowed the already developed idea from the Sumerians, and others believe that examples of China's earlier writing have just never been found. If an earlier writing were done on perishable bamboo or wood, it is possible that none survived. When Chinese writing does first appear, it is in the form of realistic pictograms carved on highly polished animal bones and turtle shells by the emperor's priests.

The priests, called shamans or diviners or oracles, used a stylus to carve the emperor's questions on the polished surfaces. The questions could range from, "Should I go hunting next Saturday?" to "Should I attack the barbarians in the north?" According to their religious beliefs, every move the ancient Chinese made could end in disaster if it displeased the gods or the ancestral spirits, so every question was important.

The diviner then applied a hot metal bar to a hole drilled in the bone. The heat caused cracks in the bone, and the design of the cracks gave the diviner the answer. After he had read the meaning, which was almost always "no," "yes," or "maybe," he wrote the answer on the bone. Tens of thousands of these bones, called oracle bones, have been discovered.

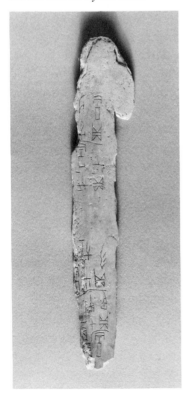

Chinese priests used oracle bones, like this one, to ask the gods and ancestral spirits for advice on actions contemplated by the emperor. The bones were heated and the answers found in cracks caused by the heat.

Logograms

Chinese pictograms are called logograms, and about fifteen hundred different ones have been found on the oracle bones. These first logograms are realistic drawings of the things they represent. The logogram of the sun looks like the sun, and the lo-

The Japanese language also uses logograms, or symbols to represent words, as these children demonstrate.

gogram of a mountain looks like a mountain. And, just like the Sumerian and Egyptian pictograms when they first appeared, each logogram represented a whole word for a person or thing. To write the word *woman*, the Chinese drew the picture of a woman. But, unlike the Sumerians and Egyptians, the Chinese never did develop their logograms into syllable or letter phonograms. Even today all Chinese logograms represent whole words.

Very shortly, the Chinese invented ideograms by designing logograms that represented idea words. With this addition, they could write, "The kite is flying," instead of just "kite." They also developed some logograms that were phonograms for the sound of whole words. This was possible because at the time they were developing their written lan-

Classic Chinese logograms have changed very little since 200 B.C., meaning that a modern Chinese scholar can read what his or her ancestors wrote two thousand years ago.

guage, most Chinese words were one-syllable words with one sound, like those of the Sumerian language. But these phonograms are always used to clarify the meaning of other logograms. They are never used alone. In a way, the Chinese phonograms are used like determinatives. The Chinese have many words that have more than one meaning. In fact, some of their words have more than fifty different meanings. Although very often it is possible to tell the meaning just from the context of the conversation, as it is in most languages, the Chinese mainly use different vocal tones in their spoken language to indicate which meaning they are using. For some meanings, the voice rises; for some, it drops; for others, the person speaks in a monotone. In their written language, phonograms are used with another logogram, one that has more than one meaning, to indicate the correct voice tone for that logogram. It is just an additional clue to which meaning is intended by the word.

Language based on meaning, not sound

The Chinese never used their phonograms alone or developed a written language based on the sounds of spoken language because they wanted their written language to depend on the meaning of the words, not on the way the words sound when they are spo-

Reading the Chinese language can be difficult, since one needs to memorize more than one thousand logograms just to read a simple story. Chinese now consists of more than fifty thousand logograms.

ken. By ensuring that all people throughout the country could communicate in the same written language, they were deliberately trying to keep their country unified. If they wrote with phonograms that were based on the sounds of one dialect, people who spoke other dialects with different sounds would not be able to read them. But everyone knew that the logogram of a horse meant "horse" no matter what a person's particular word for "horse" was or how he or she pronounced it. All Chinese citizens, no matter which of the fifty or more dialects of their language they spoke, could read the logograms. It helped to give the Chinese people a common culture.

This is still true today because the classic Chinese logograms have changed very little since 200 B.C. A modern Chinese scholar can still read what his or her ancestors wrote two thousand years ago. In fact, anyone who is willing to memorize the logograms can read them. But in order to read something very simple, it is necessary to memorize more than one thousand logograms. In all, there are now more than fifty thousand logograms. Every time a new word is added to the language (and think of all the new things that have been invented in just this century), a new logogram has to be invented. The logogram for "train," for instance, was made by combining the logograms for "fire" and "wagon."

Logograms become more abstract

The original logograms did undergo some changes, of course. Between 1500 and 200 B.C., they looked less and less like the realistic pictures the priests had carved onto the oracle bones. Lines were changed, added, and taken away. The logograms became more and more stylized. The realistic pictures turned into intricate little symbols that required the drawing of a number of separate lines and looked nothing at all like the things they represented. For example, the original logogram for "moon" looked like the drawing of a half moon (left), but today the logogram for "moon" has evolved to look like the figure on the right:

No one is sure why these changes occurred the way they did. It might have been partly the result of a need to standardize the logograms so that everyone drew them the same way every time.

In other civilizations, changes in writing style were usually due to changes in writing materials, but until 200 B.C., Chinese writing was consistently carved on hard surfaces like bone, bronze, or narrow strips of bamboo or wood. Then the Chinese invented the paintbrush. After that, writing was done with fine brushes and black ink on silk scrolls, and this change did affect the style of writing. With the ease of writing this gave them, the scribes began to pay a great deal of attention to the beauty of the logograms. Poetry and literature were judged not only by their content but also by the handwriting, and every scribe developed his own handwriting style. Logograms were considered a high form of art and were often included in paintings. From this love of line and composition in writing came calligraphy, the art of beautiful handwriting.

Chinese value written communication

Learning to write beautifully just lengthens the amount of time it takes Chinese people to learn to read and write. Today, it takes the average Chinese student ten years. It was not much different in 200

B.C. Even then, education was considered very important and was open to all boys. Learning to read and write was encouraged because writing was one of the main links among the numerous cultures. The importance of written communication may explain why China has the oldest postal system in the world. At least three thousand years ago, mail carriers were running along the rutted roads that connected China's villages and cities, delivering written messages. In 500 B.C. Confucius, a Chinese philosopher, wrote about the Imperial Post, a system of mail delivery in which horse-drawn stagecoaches arrived at specified mail stops on a regular schedule.

China also has the honor of having the oldest writing system in the world. They have used the same basic system for well over three thousand years. This system has worked well for the Chinese, and they have never felt the need to change it.

(opposite page) The Chinese philosopher Confucius wrote about the Chinese postal system, the oldest in the world, in which horse-drawn stagecoaches arrived at specified mail stops on a regular schedule.

7

The Mayans

HALFWAY AROUND THE WORLD from China, in the area called Middle America, there are few riverbanks. In this area that includes Guatemala, El Salvador, and parts of Mexico and Honduras, the advanced Mayan civilization developed. Between A.D. 250 and 900, the Mayans built terraced gardens and irrigation canals, large cities and huge pyramids, wide roads and strange, stone sculptures. Since they were farmers who depended on rain for survival, their rigid civilization was built around pleasing the gods who controlled the rain. And since it was the priests who knew how to control the gods, they had the most power.

Over hundreds of years, as the priests observed the heavens and prayed for rain, they began to see an order in the movements of the sun, moon, and stars. They saw how the movements were connected to the seasons. And they learned how to predict the rainy season, eclipses of the sun and moon, and other natural occurrences. Of course, the more they knew and the more they could predict, the more powerful they became. This motivated the Mayans to invent a system of mathematics so that they could calculate the movements of the stars. They developed a system consisting of a series of dots and dashes, using the picture of a shell to represent zero. This worked well until they began to use their mathematics to devise a

(opposite page) Mayan writing, like these hieroglyphs found in Guatemala, evolved because of the Mayan priests' obsession with time. The Mayans were the only people in the Americas to invent a writing system.

The Mayans loved elaborate ornamentation and carving. They carved strange, imaginary animals as well as gods like Kukulcan, the half-bird, half-snake god of creation, pictured here.

calendar to keep an accurate account of time. As the calendar became more and more complicated, the priests realized they needed a better way to record the days. It was the Mayan priests' obsession with time that led them to invent a writing system.

The Mayans' writing system

The Mayans are the only people in the Americas who actually invented a writing system. Although their picture writing was invented sometime after A.D. 250, thousands of years after the Sumerians invented the first picture writing, it involved the same intellectual process and is just as great an accomplishment.

The Mayans who lived between A.D. 250 and 900, at the height of the Mayan civilization, loved elaborate ornamentation. They painted their faces and bodies red or black. They pierced their earlobes, nostrils, and lips, and tattooed their bodies. They carved stone sculptures on their temples and other public buildings. Many of the carvings are of strange, imaginary animals; others are of gods, like Kukulcan, the god of creation, who was half-bird, half-snake. When the carvings were finished, the artists painted them in brilliant yellows, reds, greens, blues, and whites. This love of decoration carried over to their writing. The picture writing the Mayan priests invented was also elaborate and ornamental.

The pictograms and ideograms from Middle America are called hieroglyphs. They were named after the hieroglyphs of ancient Egypt by the people who discovered them, but they do not look like Egyptian hieroglyphs. Mayan hieroglyphs are intricate drawings of the weird, grotesque heads of humans, monsters, and gods.

The Mayans were able to write with intricately drawn hieroglyphs because, like the Egyptians, they began by carving on hard surfaces. The hieroglyphic calendars and, less frequently, other hieroglyphic writings were carved on commemorative stone mon-

The Mayans liked to draw strange, grotesque heads of humans, monsters, and gods. Their drawings were quite intricate, as is this Mayan mural. Their love of decoration carried over to their writing.

uments, temples, staircases, altars, tombs, ball-court markers, and walls all over the cities. The hieroglyphs were carved on stone, on the stucco that was plastered over many of the inside walls, and on ornaments made of jade, bone, and shell. The Mayans also painted on pottery. The writing was everywhere, but only the priests could read it. Commoners and probably most nobles never did learn to read or write, for the knowledge of writing was kept secret by the priests who wanted to keep power. To most Mayans, the hieroglyphs were magical and mysterious.

The mysterious Mayans

Mayan hieroglyphs are still somewhat of a mystery. Although experts know how to decipher the ones that relate to time and mathematics, they have not been able to decipher many of those that were used to record historical events such as wars and the reigns of kings. There are, however, far fewer of those historical writings because the hieroglyphs were used mainly to record matters relating to time, astronomy, and religion. Unlike other ancient civi-

Hieroglyphic writings were carved on commemorative stone monuments, temples, staircases, altars, tombs, and walls throughout Mayan history, as they were at this site in southern Mexico.

lizations, the Mayans did not seem to use their writing system for record-keeping. At least no business records or lists have been found or deciphered. Until the experts succeed in deciphering all the hieroglyphs, however, little will be known about Mayan writing. They do know it was read in lines from left to right, and the lines were read from top to bottom.

Most of the 750 hieroglyphs that have been found relate to time because the Mayans seem to have been particularly obsessed by time. They believed that time had no beginning or end but was a repeating cycle. When one cycle ended, another began. At the height of their civilization, they were living in the world's fourth cycle of time. The first three, they believed, had all been ended by great floods. The calendar they developed was as accurate as ours, and they did it without the use of telescopes or any of our modern equipment. By observing the heavens from their dome-topped, stone observatories, the Mayans calculated the length of the solar year, 365 days. But they divided their year into eighteen months of 20 days each, with an extra 5-day period that was considered unlucky. At the same time, they had a 260-day year that marked time for religious purposes. These two years ran side by side. A specific day on the solar calendar matched up with its corresponding day on the religious calendar only once every fifty-two years. This year during which the calendars coincided was sacred.

An impressive calendar

The Mayans also devised a second, even more impressive calendar called the long count. It set a starting point for all dates that followed, just as we date our calendar from the birth of Christ. The Mayans began their calendar with a date that corresponds to our year 3113 B.C., but no one knows why they picked that date. Experts have been able to calculate the long count dates so precisely in relation to our calendar that they can state that an event in Mayan history happened on, for example, July 6, A.D. 754.

The calendars were composed of many different, interwoven time periods. For instance, a *kin* was a day; a *uinal* was a month; a *katun* was 7,200 days. The Mayans even designated a time period called *kinchiltun* for 1,152,000,000 days. Each of those time periods had its own hieroglyph. A typical Mayan inscription would begin with a very large, introductory hieroglyph. It always had the same border, but the center was one of eighteen different hieroglyphs that represented the eighteen Mayan months, or it was the hieroglyph that represented the 5-day unlucky period. Then came hieroglyphs and number signs that told how many of each of the many different time periods had passed since their calendar began in 3113 B.C.—how many *kins,* how many *uinals,* how many *kinchiltuns,* and so on. At the end of the inscription, the priests wrote information such as the age of the moon, the name of the day for the date being commemorated, the patron deity of that date, and, occasionally, updates to the calendar.

While some Mayan hieroglyphs are simple pictograms representing things and people, most seem to be ideograms because they represent an abstract period of time, which is an idea, not a thing. Experts now believe that a few hieroglyphs are phonograms, but since they cannot read them, they cannot prove it.

Mayan inventions

In the later years of their civilization, the Mayans invented a type of paper and even books. The paper was made from the inner bark of a wild fig tree. A strip of bark about eight or nine inches high and ten to twenty feet wide was pounded until it had the consistency of cloth. This was covered with a thin coat of white lime to make the writing surface. The strips were then folded widthwise, like an accordion, into a book with pages four to six inches wide. The priests painted these books in several colors with pictures of gods and ceremonies and columns of hieroglyphs. The books, called codices, were then bound with decorated wood covers.

The Mayans built and advanced civilization in the relatively short span of about 650 years. And then, in about A.D. 1000, their civilization mysteriously collapsed. Cities were deserted. Farming stopped. No more hieroglyphs were written. For a long time, experts believed the collapse had happened suddenly because of a great disaster, such as conquest by another people or an uprising by the peasants. Evidence now seems to point to a gradual decline caused by a number of things, including numerous wars and difficulty in producing enough food for the growing population. In less than 100 years, the Mayan population dropped from about three million to less than

The Mayans watched the heavens from dome-topped, stone observatories like this one in southern Mexico.

The Mayans depicted their daily lives with hieroglyphs, ideograms, and what researchers believe are phonograms. This mural, found on a temple wall in Mexico, is one example.

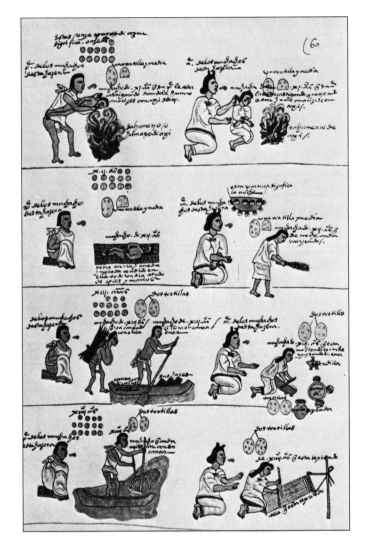

half a million. Those who remained scattered throughout Middle America where their descendants still live.

Spanish conquerors

By 1546, all of Middle America had been conquered by the Spanish. Bishop de Landa was one of the Spanish priests who arrived soon after the conquest to convert the Mayan Indians to Christianity. He was interested in the Mayan culture and wrote a book in 1566 describing how to decipher the Mayan date hieroglyphs. Without his book, those hieroglyphs might never have been read.

But de Landa, in the end, did more harm than good. The Mayans had a library in the town of Mani, on the Yucatan peninsula, that contained many books, or codices, on religion, mathematics, astronomy, astrology, and history. Because de Landa wanted to destroy the Mayan religion, and because he believed the books contained superstition and lies, he burned them all. At least he thought he did. Four books survived and are now in various museums around the world. One book contains writings on astronomy, with tables for predicting solar eclipses. Another details the influence of the planet Venus on religion and astrology. The third describes rituals and ceremonies. And the last one holds horoscopes and prophecies. None of them contains historical writings. Due to Bishop de Landa, much about the Mayan civilization will remain a mystery forever.

8

Sequoyah and the Cherokee "Alphabet"

ALL THE WRITING SYSTEMS developed during the history of mankind have taken hundreds of years to perfect and required the efforts of many people. All, that is, except one. In the early nineteenth century, a writing system was invented by one remarkable man in just a few short years. That man was a Cherokee Indian named Sequoyah.

Sequoyah did not invent writing as the Sumerians and Mayans did. He borrowed the idea of writing from the white settlers. But, since he did not know how to read and did not even understand how their system worked, his invention of a writing system was an astounding accomplishment. He single-handedly invented a system of syllable phonograms to correspond to his people's language, and that system was so well developed that his people could learn it and use it to write within days.

The Cherokee were southeastern American Indians who once lived in a huge area that now encompasses the states of North Carolina, South Carolina, Georgia, Tennessee, and Alabama. Cherokee men looked very distinctive because they wore turbans

(opposite page) A Cherokee Indian named Sequoyah borrowed the idea of writing from white settlers and, although he could not read, invented his own written language. It used syllable sound signs that corresponded to the spoken language of the Cherokee.

wrapped around their heads. After the white settlers arrived, the Cherokee adopted many of the settlers' innovations, and their nation became very prosperous. They farmed with iron plows; raised cattle, horses, and pigs; and worked as blacksmiths and operated ferryboats. But their prosperity could not save their land. Every year, more and more of it was taken over by the white settlers.

Sequoyah was born in Tennessee in about 1780. He grew up to be a very clever man. When he began making jewelry, spoons, and spurs out of the white settlers' silver coins, he became the first Cherokee silversmith. After he invented paintbrushes made of hair without ever having seen one before, he became an excellent artist. He also worried a great deal about his people. He saw the way they were losing their land because the white settlers were so powerful, and he wanted to make the Cherokee just as powerful so they could keep their land. Finally, he decided that it was books, what the Cherokee called "talking leaves," that gave the white settlers their power. So in 1809 he set out to develop a writing system.

Sequoyah's daring experiment

Sequoyah did not know that such a thing had never been done before. No one person had ever just sat down and invented a writing system, especially a person who knew only one language and could not read. Perhaps it is just as well, for he began without truly knowing what a huge task he had set for himself. At first he tried to invent a pictogram for each word in the Cherokee language, which is how many other writing systems had begun. But after he had drawn thousands of pictograms he could not even remember himself what they all meant. Undaunted, he struggled for years with the overwhelming task he was determined to accomplish. He was so single-minded that his wife felt neglected and got so angry with him one day that she burned all the records of his work, which he had written on strips of bark.

Most people would have become very discouraged at this point, but Sequoyah just went on working. In fact, losing his records helped him. He started rethinking the whole problem and came up with an improved system. He decided to use syllable sound signs, or phonograms. First, he recorded every syllable sound in the Cherokee language and discovered that eighty-six phonograms could be combined to form all the words. Although he had no idea what the letters in the English alphabet meant, he had seen them somewhere and decided to use them for his syllable signs. He chose the capital letters and by turning some upside down and inventing others, he finally came up with eighty-six signs. Now he could write his native language.

The magic of the alphabet

But his problems were only beginning. His people refused to have anything to do with this "magic." He decided to provide them with a public demonstration. Sequoyah sat down with his six-year-old daughter, Ayogu, and taught her to read his signs. This done, he went off to a trial without her and wrote down everything that happened. Then he called a meeting with the Arkansas Cherokee chiefs and had Ayogu read his notes in front of them. The chiefs were totally amazed, but unfortunately, they were even more convinced the signs were magical. They still did not want anything to do with them.

But one chief, Big Rattling Gourd, thought all night about what had happened and went to see Sequoyah the next day. He realized what a remarkable invention the writing system was, and that gave Sequoyah the courage to ask for another public test. He got permission to teach the signs to some of the tribe's young men. Then the chiefs tested Sequoyah's students by separating them into two groups. They sent the first group out of the room while they dictated messages to the second group. Then they called the first group back into the room and had them read what the second group had written. This test worked. The Cherokees in Arkansas were so delighted with their own "talking leaves," they gave Sequoyah a huge feast and had a medal made in his honor.

Sequoyah had invented a writing system so simple that his people could learn to read and write in two or three days. They wrote signs all over their cabin walls and fences. But so far only the Cherokees in Arkansas knew about his system. So he wrote messages to his people in the East and carried them there himself in 1824. The rest of the Cherokee nation eagerly accepted his writing system, and within a matter of months, the entire nation could read and write.

Unfortunately, the power that writing gave to the Cherokee nation was never enough to withstand the greater power of the United States, no matter how

The discovery of gold in Georgia heralded the end of Sequoyah's writing system. Thousands of acres of land were taken from the Cherokees, who were forced to move west.

hard the Cherokees tried. For example, by 1827, the Cherokees had adopted a constitution based on the United States Constitution. By 1828, they had a printing press and were publishing a newspaper, the *Cherokee Phoenix.* Their progress was remarkable. Never before had a nation matured so fast. But gold was discovered on their land in Georgia, and before the gold rush was over, Georgia had taken over thousands of acres of Cherokee land.

Writing cannot save the Cherokee nation

And then came the final blow. The United States Congress passed a law in 1830 that ordered all the Cherokees and other Indian tribes in the east to move west of the Mississippi River. For the next eight years, Sequoyah and most other Cherokees refused to move, so in 1838 the government gathered them together and marched seventeen thousand of them to the West. Four thousand Cherokees died of hunger, exposure, and disease on the trail, a trip they call "The Trail of Tears." Sequoyah himself died in 1843.

Thousands of Cherokees still live in Oklahoma and North Carolina, but they now read and write English, and Sequoyah's syllable writing system is just a memory. His remarkable achievement did not, however, go completely unnoticed by the United States government. In recognition of what he had done, the amazing giant sequoia trees discovered in California were named after him, and Sequoia National Park was established to protect those trees.

In recognition of Sequoyah's accomplishment, huge trees found in California—and the national park created to protect them—were named after him. Today, sequoia trees stand tall in Sequoia National Park.

Erfindung der Schreibekunst
in Phœnizien.

Epilogue

BY 1700 B.C., the stage was set for the emergence of the alphabet. Traders and diplomats had spread the knowledge of Sumerian cuneiform and Egyptian hieroglyphs to other civilizations throughout the Middle East. Those civilizations had adapted the syllable and letter phonograms to fit the sounds of their own spoken languages. There was more and more need for writing in government, business, religion, and the arts, and the scribes were constantly seeking ways to improve their writing systems.

One civilization had a particular need for a fast, flexible, easy way to write because it was located in what is now the country of Syria at the eastern end of the Mediterranean, the main crossroads for the ancient world. These people called themselves Canaanites, but we call them Phoenicians. Their cities were centers for the bustling trade that operated on both the sea and land routes between the Asian and African continents. The Phoenicians had a great talent for manufacturing and trade. They did not write inscriptions and literature; they kept records of business transactions. And they did not want to hire a professional scribe each time they had to create an invoice or a contract or a deed. They wanted a system that was quick and easy to learn so that their clerks could do it all.

The Phoenicians experimented with both hieroglyphs and cuneiform as they searched for the best

(opposite page) Phoenician civilization had a particular need for a fast, flexible way to write because their cities were commercial centers. So they experimented with hieroglyphs and cuneiform writing, as depicted in this mural.

way to conduct their business. Then, according to many experts, one ingenious scribe hit upon the answer. He developed the first system of writing in which all the signs were sound signs for individual letters. He had invented an alphabet, and that Phoenician alphabet is the precursor of all the alphabets in use today.

(opposite page) The Phoenicians developed the first system of writing in which all the signs were sound signs for individual letters. This clay tablet, found in Syria, carries most of the letters of the Phoenician alphabet, which is the precursor of alphabets used today.

Glossary

aborigines: The dark-skinned people who are the earliest known inhabitants of Australia.

archaeologist: An expert who excavates and studies the remains of historic or prehistoric peoples and their cultures.

Ashurbanipal: A Babylonian king who died in about 626 B.C.

Babylonians: The people who lived in Babylonia just north of Sumer and conquered the Sumerians in 1763 B.C.

calligraphy: The art of beautiful penmanship, highly decorated handwriting.

chasqis: An Incan messenger.

city-state: A city with its own power and authority governed only by its own ruler.

codices: Mayan books.

Confucius: A Chinese philosopher and teacher who lived from approximately 551 to 478 B.C.

cuneiform: The Sumerian system of writing by pressing a stylus into clay.

demotic: A fast, shorthand type of Egyptian writing that developed from hieratic and was adopted by the common people for everyday use.

determinative: A sign placed in front of a phonogram by the Sumerians and Egyptians to indicate how to read the phonogram correctly.

dialect: A regional variety of a particular language that differs in pronunciation, vocabulary, and grammar from the other regional varieties of that language.

Egyptologist: An expert on ancient Egypt.

fossil: Anything remaining from an earlier geologic period in the history of the earth.

hieratic: An Egyptian writing system that developed from the hieroglyphs as a faster and easier method of writing.

hieroglyph: The name given by the Greeks to Egyptian writing signs.

116

Homo sapiens: The species of primates to which humans belong, characterized by a brain averaging eighty-five cubic inches, by walking on two limbs, by language, and by the use of complex tools.

ibex: A wild mountain goat with long, curved horns.

ideogram: A pictogram or picture word that represents an idea rather than the concrete thing it pictures.

Incas: A tribe of Indians who lived along the west coast of South America and expanded their culture into a highly developed civilization between A.D. 200 and 1440.

Iroquois League: A political organization formed by all the Woodland Indian tribes of New York and Pennsylvania to keep peace among themselves and other tribes.

katun: The Mayan word for a time period of 7,200 days.

kin: The Mayan word for day.

kinchiltun: The Mayan word for a time period of 1,152,000,000 days.

Kukulcan: The Mayan god of creation who was half-bird and half-snake.

last ice age: The last time glaciers covered much of Europe, Asia, and North America, roughly from 70,000-9,000 B.C.

logogram: The name given to Chinese pictograms.

long count: The complex Mayan calendar that set a starting point at 3113 B.C. for all Mayan dates.

memory aid: A prewriting device that forms a permanent record.

message stick: A type of memory aid made from carving notches on a stick.

Middle America: The name given to the area that now includes the countries of Guatemala and El Salvador and parts of Mexico and Honduras.

nomadic: The culture of nomads who regularly move from place to place in search of food.

ocher: A natural, earthy mixture containing iron that ranges from yellow to red in color and is used as pigment for painting.

oracle bone: A bone or turtle shell used by Chinese shamans to ask and answer a question to the gods.

papyrus: A form of paper the Egyptians made from papyrus reeds.

phonetic writing: A system of writing based on the sounds of spoken language.

phonogram: A pictogram that represents the sound of the word for the thing pictured.

pictogram: A picture word, a picture that represents the word for the thing pictured.

picture story: A storytelling picture, a drawing of an event that is meant to tell the story of that event.

prehistoric: The period of time before recorded history, before history could be recorded in writing.

quipu: A complicated memory aid invented by the Incas that used knots tied onto bunches of string.

quipucamayoc: An Incan knot keeper, an educated Inca who could knot quipus and read them.

rebus: A writing game using pictograms in which pictures of sound alike words are substituted for words which have no easy pictures, e.g., bee for be.

Rosetta stone: A stone discovered in Egypt in 1799 which contained the same inscription in Greek, hieroglyphs, and demotic, enabling Egyptologists to decipher hieroglyphs.

sachem: A wise man who was a member of the Iroquois League.

scribe: A member of the educated class whose ability to read and write gave him power and influence in his society.

shaman: A priest, a tribal member who acts as an intermediary between the natural and supernatural worlds; also called diviner and oracle.

static: A design that looks fixed and stationary, showing little or no movement or vitality.

stela (pl. stelae): A commemorative stone monument inscribed with writing.

stylized: A design that conforms to a particular style and is similar to all the other designs in that style.

stylus: A reed pen used by the Sumerians to write on clay; any of a number of pointed, pen-shaped writing instruments made of metal or bone.

Sumer: The land of the Sumerians in what is now the country of Iran; the area where human civilization first developed and true writing was first invented.

Tigris River: A Middle Eastern river in what is now the country of Iran; the first civilization grew up along its banks and those of its neighboring river, the Euphrates.

totem pole: A pole carved and painted by the Indians of the northwest coast of North America to represent the symbols of their clan or tribe.

uinal: The Mayan word for month.

wampum: A memory aid made from seashells that was used to keep records of the Iroquois Leagues' treaties.

winter count: A picture story painted on a hide by the Plains Indians each winter as a memory aid to commemorate the past year.

Chronology of
Early Writing

c. 300,000 B.C.	Homo sapiens appears on earth
c. 100,000-40,000 B.C.	People develop capacity for speech
c. 35,000 B.C.	Cave paintings appear in Europe
c. 9000 B.C.	Last cave paintings
c. 8500 B.C.	Animals domesticated in Middle East
c. 8000 B.C.	Rock art appears in eastern Spain
c. 7500 B.C.	Wheat first cultivated in Middle East
c. 4000 B.C.	First city-states develop in Sumer
c. 3500 B.C.	Sumerians use pictograms to identify property
c. 3100 B.C.	Sumerians invent first picture writing
c. 3000 B.C.	Egyptians use hieroglyphic writing
c. 2900 B.C.	Egyptians invent papyrus
c. 2800 B.C.	Sumerians invent phonograms
c. 2400 B.C.	Sumerian writing becomes cuneiform
c. 2000 B.C.	Sumerians invent envelope Rock art in eastern Spain ceases
c. 1700-1400 B.C.	Phoenicians invent first complete alphabet
c. 1500 B.C.	Picture writing appears suddenly in China
c. 1000 B.C.	Chinese develop mail delivery system
c. 800 B.C.	Greeks develop modern alphabet, with vowels
c. 700 B.C.	Demotic writing brings literacy to Egyptian people

c. 200 B.C.	Modern Chinese logograms developed
75 A.D.	Last cuneiform inscription
c. 300 A.D.	Mayans invent hieroglyphic writing
394 A.D.	Last Egyptian hieroglyphic inscription
c. 1000 A.D.	Last Mayan inscription
1822 A.D.	Egyptian hieroglyphs deciphered
1824 A.D.	Sequoyah's syllable alphabet used by Cherokees

Suggestions for Further Reading

Gordon C. Baldwin, *Talking Drums to Written Word*. New York: Norton, 1970.

Hans Georg Bandi, *The Art of the Stone Age: 40,000 Years of Rock Art*. New York: Crown, 1961.

William Cahn and Rhoda Cahn, *The Story of Writing*. New York: Harvey House, 1963.

Lionel Casson, *Ancient Egypt*. Alexandria, VA: Time-Life Books, 1965.

Lionel Casson, *Daily Life in Ancient Egypt*. New York: American Heritage Publishing Co., 1975.

Edward Chiera, *They Wrote on Clay*. Chicago: University of Chicago Press, 1938.

Robert Claiborne, *The Birth of Writing*. New York: Time-Life Books, 1974.

Alfred Fairbank, *The Story of Handwriting*. New York: Watson-Guptill, 1970.

Sydney Fletcher, *The American Indian*. New York: Grosset & Dunlap, 1954.

Albertine Gaur, *A History of Writing*. New York: Scribner's, 1985.

Enrico Guidoni and Roberto Magni, *Monuments of Civilization: The Andes*. New York: Grosset & Dunlap, 1977.

Evan Hadingham, *Secrets of the Ice Age: The World of the Cave Artists*. New York: Walker, 1979.

Christine Hobson, *The World of the Pharaohs*. New York: Thames & Hudson, 1987.

Donald Jackson, *The Story of Writing*. New York: Taplinger, 1981.

Loren McIntyre, *The Incredible Incas and Their Timeless Land*. Washington, DC: National Geographic Society, 1975.

Douglas Mazonowicz, *Voices from the Stone Age: A Search for Cave and Canyon Art*. New York: Thomas Y. Crowell, 1974.

Frances Rogers, *Painted Rock to Printed Page*. New York: J. B. Lippincott, 1960.

Edward H. Schafer, *Ancient China*. New York: Time-Life Books, 1967.

Ann Sieveking, *The Cave Artists*. London: Thames & Hudson, 1979.

George E. Stuart and Gene S. Stuart, *The Mysterious Maya*. Washington, DC: National Geographic Society, 1977.

Time-Life Books. *China*. Amsterdam: Time-Life Books, 1984.

C. B. F. Walker, *Reading the Past: Cuneiform*. Berkeley: University of California Press, 1987.

Works Consulted

Kenneth Allen, *One Day in Tutankhamen's Egypt.* New York: Abelard-Schuman, 1974.

Norman Bate, *When Cave Men Painted.* New York: Scribner's, 1963.

Barbara L. Beck, *The Ancient Maya.* New York: Franklin Watts, 1983.

Wendy Boase, *Ancient Egypt.* New York: Gloucester Press, 1978.

Alice Dickinson, *The First Book of Stone Age Man.* New York: Franklin Watts, 1962.

Robert (Gray-Wolf) Hofsinde, *The Indian's Secret World.* New York: William Morrow, 1955.

Penelope Hughes-Stanton, *See Inside an Ancient Chinese Town.* New York: Warwick Press, 1979.

Norma Jean Katan, *Hieroglyphs*: *The Writing of Ancient Egypt.* New York: Atheneum, 1981.

R. J. Unstead, *See Inside an Egyptian Town.* New York: Warwick Press, 1986.

Victor W. von Hagen, *The Incas: People of the Sun.* New York: The World Publishing Co., 1961.

Richard L. Walker, *Ancient China and Its Influence in Modern Times.* New York: Franklin Watts, 1969.

Index

About the Author

Lois Warburton earned her Masters degree in education at Clark University in Worcester, Massachusetts. Her previous published works include nonfiction articles, newspaper and magazine columns, and short stories. She is a past president of The Wordwright, a firm providing writing services to authors, businesses, and individuals. Ms. Warburton is now retired.

Picture Credits